The Dandelions of Woodlawn Avenue

The Dandelions of Woodlawn Avenue

✦

"A woman's search for meaning and purpose in life"

Jo Singel

iUniverse, Inc.

New York Lincoln Shanghai

The Dandelions of Woodlawn Avenue
"A woman's search for meaning and purpose in life"

iUniverse books may be ordered through booksellers or by contacting:

iUniverse
2021 Pine Lake Road, Suite 100
Lincoln, NE 68512
www.iuniverse.com
1-800-Authors (1-800-288-4677)

ISBN-13: 978-0-595-36092-5 (pbk)
ISBN-13: 978-0-595-80539-6 (ebk)
ISBN-10: 0-595-36092-0 (pbk)
ISBN-10: 0-595-80539-6 (ebk)

Printed in the United States of America

To my son Jonathan, the miracle in my life, so that he can know where he came from.

Contents

Acknowledgements

To family and friends who have helped me in the editing of this book, I am eternally grateful. Their assistance and support during the two years I worked on the manuscript will always remain a treasured memory. My husband, Don, and my son, Jonathan read numerous drafts and listened to the stories that comprise the book, providing ideas and feedback. They helped me make this venture a reality.

To my cousin Sofia, I thank and am grateful for her help in reading through my draft and providing me with valuable ideas and honest feedback. She was always a source of positive support and helped to keep me on an even keel emotionally. I appreciate her wisdom.

To my friend Barbara Del Negro who approached the reading of the manuscript with her heart and soul. Her encouragement, support, creative ideas and intuitive sensibility was invaluable.

To my friends Anika Gakovic and Paul Gallico, I thank for taking the time to read the manuscript and giving me insight into how to stay truthful to my concept. Anika encouraged me to express the emotional side of myself. Paul used his curiosity to help me go to a deeper level in my writing.

To my friend Harriet Maphet who supported me with her kindness and thoughtfulness as I worked on the draft during my summer vacations in Ocean Grove, New Jersey. She made sure I was never without food and other sustenance.

To my friends Ellen Reilly, Cecilia Matthews, Debra Rosenblum, David Muha, Rose Marie, and many others who provided encouragement through their interest and involvement in my efforts to portray a true picture of my stories. Mostly, they listened, which is what every writer ultimately wants and needs.

And finally, to Angie and Bill at the Laingdon Hotel in Ocean Grove, New Jersey, whose generosity I am eternally thankful for. They listened to my stories, made me coffee and breakfast and did whatever they could to make me feel comfortable and at home. I always felt safe and cared for; they provided me with a "home away from home".

INTRODUCTION

I've been writing this book for the better part of my life, beginning with my first diary entry when I was eight years old. I wrote a piece called, "How to Live Your Life", by Josephine Pagano. It was a numbered check-list of important to do's such as, say your prayers, brush your teeth, and love your mother and father. It was simple, concise and direct. Then, a few short years later, things became more complicated. There were Girl Scout events, movies, books, and conversations—quickly followed by stories of boy friends, dates, broken hearts, proms and dreams of life beyond high school.

From the recording of events to the expression of feelings and emotions, the young girl's thoughts evolved into an adolescent's fears, concerns and challenges.

Finally, the woman's voice emerged. Journal after journal entry, and page by page, a life was recorded. Sometimes written in minute detail, oftentimes scribbled hastily on pieces of paper in short, terse sentences, emotional moments and everyday activities were described

Over the years, I wrote letters to various people in my life seldom sharing them but keeping them in folders. I don't know why I never sent them; it was what I did.

I always wanted to write a book—I thought about it, dreamed about it but never did what was necessary until now.

I spent the past several years reading, reviewing and then assessing all that I had written up until this point.

Stories began to emerge. Some were chosen and some were not.

These are my stories. They are not intended to provide help or advice. The book has been a catharsis and a personal exploration. It may, however, provide some inspiration or motivation to the reader.

Preface

Decoding a life, story by story, letter by letter—bits, pieces and fragments—uncovered, exposed, and revealed—slowly, painstakingly—life running off the pages—unable to remain between the margins and borders, defying formatting and rules—releasing emotions and feelings, relentlessly expanding, demanding voice and space—unheard of expressions—surprises—creating its own redemption along the way—line by line, word by word—forming mountains, hills, gullies, and ruts. All that a life is and is not. Try to control it and you kill it. Let it loose to run free and it takes advantage, going off in every direction. What to do with a life that wants to live free? How do words describe it? How can a page contain it?

The Dandelions of Woodlawn Avenue

o o o o o o o o o o o o o o o o o o o o o o o o o o o o o o o o

"My thoughts take me back to the beginning, to the innocent time, the time when there is no such thing as time, when time is marked by meal times, bath time, brushing teeth time, snack time and play time. When I think about the dandelions on our patch of grass on Woodlawn Avenue, I smile a contented smile filled with a feeling of peace. A soft, slow, gaze takes me back to life on a small town street in America in the 1950s.

There's a place that nearly everyone remembers when thinking back over their childhood. It is a special place that may no longer exist but is just as poignant, vivid and real as if it were visited only yesterday. We can always return to this place in our minds and hearts—pulling memories at will—hearing the sounds, remembering the smells, and feeling the emotions that engaged us."

FIRST MEMORY OF JOY

When I was six years old, my family moved to Woodlawn Avenue in Upper Darby, Pennsylvania. It was a big move for us. We had previously lived on Robinson Street in West Philadelphia. My aunt, uncle and cousins were down the street from us on the same city block. My grandparents and other family members were a short trolley car ride away. Robinson Street was the first house my parents bought when they were married. The house on Woodlawn Avenue would be their last. They would raise two children there and after each of my parents died, the funeral car carrying them to the cemetery would drive by in a final farewell.

As a newly transplanted six year-old, the house on Woodlawn Avenue was beautiful and full of mystery. It was significantly bigger than our home on Robinson Street and there was plenty of space to roam and play.

The town of Upper Darby had an interesting history. Settled by Quakers in 1786, it had been home to many of Philadelphia's most influential and important families, such as the famed botanist John Bartram, the Sellers' family who donated a beautiful library to the town, the investor Christopher Fallon and several well-known abolitionists. It was an old and established neighborhood. There were small Tudor-style homes, single and semi-detached houses with wide front porches, lawns, and tall trees with a few beautiful weeping willows gracing its wide streets.

Aside from its historical and esteemed beginnings, the homes were built on the side of a hill creating great sledding in winter. I remember many fun-filled days riding bikes, ice-skating on the nearby creek, playing ball, foraging for wild berries and just plain being lazy on summer afternoons with nothing more to do than drinking fresh-made lemonade and cooling off from the spray of a garden hose.

For the first time in my life, I had a patch of land to call my own. I recall the day we moved into the new house. The first thing I saw was the grassy side lawn covered with the most beautiful yellow flowers. I'd been to city parks and playgrounds but it was not the same. This was mine. Although the lawn had become overgrown with weeds due to neglect, I didn't care. I didn't expect a neat and tidy garden. What I experienced was a wild jungle full of many interesting opportunities for exploration and discovery. There was a large, old spruce tree with a bed of nettles under it—just waiting for a small body to find refuge. There was no asphalt or constant sound of cars streaming by or of people walking and talking on the sidewalks.

I would be kept busy for the next few years—picking red berries for my dolls tea parties, searching for raspberries, sledding down the driveway on snowy winter days and bouncing a ball against the side of the garage. These were the things a little girl did when she had a patch of lawn and a garden filled with flowers.

And so there I was on my first day in our new house, walking into the middle of this jumbled lawn. I did what came naturally and without much forethought. I laid flat on my back looking up at the sky. Maybe it was the bright yellow flowers that attracted my attention. I knew them only by their presence, not yet having a name to distinguish them. What I recall is the yellow glow sitting just above the line of the grass. I felt as though I were lying on a sea of gold. That moment was my first memory of joy. Surrounded by dandelions and buttercups—all their small faces, like mine, turned up to soak in the warmth of that bright sun. I gathered those dandelions by the handful and offered them as my first gift to the household.

I was soon to learn, however, that dandelions were considered an undesirable weed. People in the suburbs were repulsed by the dandelions. They were an unsightly nuisance and much time and money was spent getting rid of them.

Here we were at last, in the land of my father's dreams, on a street with perfectly groomed green lawns and "crab-grass" lurking beneath the surface—ready to spring up, bloom and spread their seeds in the wind. And as fast as it's pulled, poisoned, burned or destroyed, there's more crab grass to take its place—ready and waiting to sprout, as hardy as ever.

In many ways, my family was as unwelcome to that neighborhood as were those dandelions. Many of the first generation Italian immigrants were considered a scourge. We adapted quickly but not before experiencing the disapproval and indignation of those around us who didn't understand our behavior, habits or rituals. But, like the dandelions, we planted strong and hardy roots, slowly establishing our place in the land of opportunity, striving like everyone else to fulfill the American dream. It was a struggle, but with time and practice the women and children who were uprooted from their relatives and families in the city quickly managed to learn a new way of living. Maybe it was the promise of those Hoover vacuum cleaners, refrigerators and a room for a proper dining set that encouraged the women and mothers to dutifully, yet reluctantly, follow their husbands.

In the city, these women wore house dresses purchased from trucks or door-to-door salesmen. While their husbands were at work, their hair was pinned up in curlers and their nylon stockings were comfortably rolled down their legs just above the ankle. During the summer months, electric fans whirred in the background. Window shades were drawn low to block out the mid-day sun, leaving the rooms cool and slightly darkened. It was peaceful and quiet. The women sat on porches or steps, while the children were tucked into their beds for afternoon naps.

The wash, before washing machines, was scrubbed in tubs with aluminum boards and strong soap. It hung in small yards, close to the fig and peach trees. The steps in front of the house were cleaned every morning. Pots of water washed away the previous day's debris into the street.

Ice was delivered in carts, pulled by horses, clumping down stone laid streets.

The fruit and vegetable guys yelled out their presence from trucks struggling to make their way down narrow streets. Women bought the ingredients for that evening's supper fresh from trucks or grocery stands.

These sights, sounds, smells, noises and distinctions of the city were nowhere to be found in the suburbs. Nevertheless, my family, much like the hardy weed, the dandelion, survived just as their ancestors had done before them. Besides, without the dandelion, how would a little girl dream and make wishes, if she didn't have those white puff balls to blow on and scatter to the wind?

Liberating Others/Imprisoning Ourselves

○ ○

"Is all learning about having to do it the hard way? Why does it sometimes take a deep plunge into cold water to wake us up? I call those times, diving moments".

GETTING SIGNS

Is it possible that we receive signs of coming events in our lives? Do the "diving moments" arrive suddenly and unannounced or might there be hints of things to come? Does the future reveal itself to us in strange, irrational and inexplicable ways? Do we get "warning signs ahead"? And if so, how do we make sense of them?

On September 1, 2001, I was traveling with my husband to Penn State University where he would be attending a football game. I wasn't planning on joining him but instead would spend the day in the downtown shopping area. For us, this was a typical way to spend a football weekend in State College. But on this particular weekend there were no Inns, Bed & Breakfast or motel rooms available at State College. The only room my husband could find was in a town called Montoursville located thirty miles away from Penn State. We decided it was close enough and I'd stay there for the day. My husband would return in the evening after the game had ended. I could have a day of peace and quiet and do some shopping in the town. It sounded like a good plan and a way to de-stress from the intensity of living in Manhattan.

So there I was in Montoursville for a day of rest. I left the Bed & Breakfast in the morning and headed toward the center of the town to explore, have lunch and write in my journal. It was a beautiful day and I was looking forward to relaxing. I soon noticed how friendly and hospitable the people were in the town. I'd say unusually so. I couldn't quite put my finger on it, but to me the town felt special. People were very pleasant and extra polite, waiting patiently at crosswalks for pedestrians, saying hello to any and all who passed by. I'd visited small towns before, but there was a remarkable calmness here. What was it about this place that made it so unique?

Sometime during the morning my husband and I had passed the town high school as we made our way toward the Inn. I had noticed that there was a very large statue of a stone angel in the middle of a well-kept circular lawn in front of the school. It was the kind of statue you'd more likely see in a cemetery overlooking a mausoleum. Surrounding this big statue were stone benches. It was a very peaceful scene. But I thought it looked kind of odd—being that the angel was in front of a high school. Curious, I thought I'd visit the school after I enjoyed a leisurely lunch. Since my interest was piqued, I wanted to solve the mystery of why an angel had been placed there.

As I sat in a small coffee shop in downtown Montoursville I made some notes in my journal:

"I am here for a reason, sitting on a green stool in a small coffee shop at the counter. There's a strong feeling of bygone times as though I landed in this odd little place from some time in the future. How incredible! Just visiting doesn't have much meaning; you need to live in a place to really know it. I'm remembering our neighborhood in Upper Darby with the corner drug store...floats, sundaes and phosphates. I remember summers riding my bike, going to Upper Darby Library, playing baseball, making woven baskets in the arts and crafts barn. I spent quite a bit of time alone, in my earlier years."

I continued writing:

"Things are perfect just the way they are
Any other way wouldn't work
We are born into the unknown, fresh, with no memories of anything before that time
We don't know when we're going to die, so we must live our lives in the best way we know
Without knowing
As it should be
That way there is unlimited possibility ahead
And free will has a say
I do believe that we are here to learn about ourselves
It's good that we come into the world not knowing and pretty much leave in the same way.
I do believe that we create our reality."

That's what I wrote in my journal, sitting in the coffee shop that afternoon in Montoursville. It's something I'm prone to do especially when alone with no one to talk with or anything to read. It was a strange, rambling jumble of words that I didn't give much thought to at the time. It all sounded rather cryptic. I left the luncheonette and made my way down the streets of the small town. I wandered over to the high school and approached the eight foot tall stone angel.

There was an inscription etched in marble in the base of the statue. As I read the words that were written, I felt an overwhelming sense of astonishment and sorrow. The statue was a memorial honoring twenty-one high school students who had lost their lives on July 1, 1996. They were onboard TWA Flight 800 on their way to Paris when their plane crashed off of the coast of Long Island, New York. In a small town, that was an enormous loss, touching everyone, even the unsuspecting people who visited there.

The inscription on the memorial read:

"On Sunday evening, July 21, 1996, a cloud in the form of an angel appeared above the Montoursville High School. At the angel's left were twenty-one smaller white clouds. At first in a circle, then appearing in two straight rows.
Two small rainbows appeared and arched over the Montoursville community. The sky was unusually calm that evening, and was a beautiful shade of blue. A smaller dove-shaped cloud formed and the sky became a magnificent color pink and blue clearing as sunset arrived.
Many who witnessed these formations felt a calm inner peace. As word spread throughout the community of these events, an overwhelming sense of spiritual support developed. The angel became a symbol that linked the community to those aboard flight 800. This image captured on film by a local resident is believed by many to have been a sign that communicated the well being of our loved ones."

The memorial was built on the site of an old Indian burial ground. It was a lasting and powerful tribute to those lost lives. Finally, I had an answer to my earlier question. The town was special. A tragedy had occurred that was swift, unexpected, and difficult to comprehend. Everyone mourned. There was no escape from the emotion created by the deep loss, not even for outsiders, like myself.

During the remainder of the day, I reached out to a few shop owners and the woman who ran our Inn. I spoke with each of them about the tragedy. They all shared with me how the loss had impacted everyone in the town. Montoursville has never been the same. Some of the town's people moved away. This town had "a diving moment" and I found myself a bystander to the aftermath of their tragedy. The enormity of their loss was unmistakable. It hung heavily in the air. And I left perplexed.

Why was I in this town on this particular weekend in September and drawn as a moth to the flame, to that stone angel? A couple of years later I read my journal entry of that day and marveled at the strangeness and the mystery of our lives. As they say, even though we can't see the stars in the light of day, they are still there. I believe there are things that happen to us that we can't explain with our rational minds. It is the beauty and mystery of life at work in our everyday lives.

Ten days later, I was sitting on my bed on the eve of September 11, 2001 and wrote an entry in my journal: "Have no fear. It will be ok. There is nothing to fear." I had an ominous feeling that something very big and very bad was heading our way. I had shared this feeling with a good friend during the day and a week later she reminded me of what I had said to her. The memory of Montoursville lingered. Given the nature of my journal entry on September 1, was I getting some kind of sign? As I noted that day, everything in our lives can change so quickly and unexpectedly. The only thing we can count on is the moment in which we're living. Surely, when those children and adults set out for Paris in July, 1996, everyone was happy and joyous about the trip. When people set out for work in downtown Wall Street on September 11, 2001, their thoughts were of the day and the tasks and activities ahead: What phone calls do I need to return, how am I going to complete that assignment, what will I have for breakfast? The mundane thoughts of everyday things comprise the rhythm and flow of our lives. Sons, daughters, husbands, wives, walked out the door—some never to return. Others did arrive back home after their journeys, never to be quite the same again.

The unexpected interfered with the world of normal and what was average became extraordinary.

I'm left holding a bag of questions marked "why". Do we receive "signs" or are these stories that comprise our lives one endless stream of events with little connection to one another other than that they just happen? Are the things that happen to us based on luck—good or bad—or are we in a place and at a particular time for a reason? Are we there to "see" something, to witness, give testimony to or provide proof of evidence to something—beyond our normal, human capacity for reasoning and understanding? Is there a language of symbols, metaphors and signs on the path of life that we overlook in our haste to keep up, stay ahead, do more, have more, be more? Are we missing something important and if so, what is it? And what do we do to make sense of it once we "see" it?

DIVING MOMENTS

I am a first-generation Italian-American. I feel very fortunate to be reaping the benefits of my Italian-born father's hard work and dedication. I also carry with me his dissatisfaction, sense of duty, fears, phobias and dreams. The first five decades of my life consisted of the normal amount of joys, sorrows, and disappointments.

I remembered my father's stories but they were too distant and far removed from my reality for me to notice their influence. Was I so focused on fulfilling the dreams he had for me that I hadn't reflected on my own motivations and desires? On the other hand, had I spent much time questioning his? Regardless, as I've learned, life has a way of grabbing our attention—with sometimes subtle or not so subtle warnings, surprises or as some people might call them "accidents". I prefer to see those events as "diving moments" that plunge you into the cold, deep water, forcing you to pause and reflect on where you are and what's important to you.

My "diving moment" arrived shortly upon moving to the East Village of Manhattan. My husband and I had spent the previous twenty years living in the suburbs of Morristown, New Jersey. We were back in Manhattan, "home" again in the city we left to start and raise a family. For Don and I, there was no better place to spend the next part of our lives.

I remember it was one of those typically beautiful late summer days when I awoke to the sound of the alarm clock and followed my normal routine. I showered, drank a cup of coffee, dressed, packed my briefcase and said a hasty goodbye to my husband before bolting for the subway. I was on my way to work in downtown Wall Street and was running behind schedule. A friend and former colleague of mine whom I hadn't seen in a long time would be waiting for me. I was on automatic pilot. A few minutes after boarding the "R" train and heading downtown toward the World Trade Center (WTC), I recall glancing at my watch. It was 8:52 a.m. and we were stopped at the City Hall station. The ride was unusually rocky and I noticed that the passengers were exchanging anxious glances.

As I recollect, there were many clues that something was amiss. There were police escorting people out of the subway station as they made their way from the train. In the subway car, a young mother reached over to her daughter who was sitting by her side. She said, "Honey stay close to me. This is going to be a bumpy ride." Shortly afterwards, the conductor announced we would be bypassing the

WTC/Cortlandt Street station due to a "smoke situation" and would instead proceed to Rector Street and onto Bowling Green. I decided to exit at Rector Street. It was an unfamiliar station and I wasn't sure where it would land me relative to my office building. As we passed the WTC stop I noticed that the platform was emptied of people except for a single transit worker rousting a man who was asleep on one of the benches. Being intent on reaching my destination I wanted to exit the subway as close to the WTC as possible.

I wasn't thinking about what might be happening to cause the disruption in service, the presence of police and the empty WTC platform. As soon as I exited the subway station and stepped onto the street, I saw thousands of pieces of paper flying in the air. I thought to myself, "Is there some kind of ticker tape parade going on today that I didn't know about?" Then I noticed that the papers were on fire. Now I was alert and paying attention to my surroundings.

Fire engines, ambulances, and people were running in every direction—there was complete pandemonium on the streets. Despite the fact that I could barely move on the sidewalk, I stubbornly pushed ahead toward the WTC and the office building where I worked, two short blocks away from the Trade Center Concourse. Finally, no longer able to get past the crowds streaming toward me, I retraced my steps and headed south of the WTC.

I was determined to find another way around the turmoil to reach my destination. As I was walking, I noticed a middle-aged black man in a white tee shirt and jeans standing in the doorway of a small, darkened bar. He was openly and hysterically weeping. I made my way toward him as though in a trance and put my arm over his broad shoulders. It was as though I were swimming in very choppy ocean waters and attempting to reach someone who was struggling to keep his head above water. I could sense this man was close to drowning.

> I asked him "What happened? Why are you crying?" and he responded, "They did it! They finally did it!"

He pointed his forefinger toward the small-screen TV on the ceiling as he walked into the bar. He kept repeating, "They finally did it. They finally did it." I followed closely behind him and made my way toward the TV, mesmerized by the images of the one Tower spewing flames and billowing black smoke just a couple of blocks away from where we were standing. I could never have predicted what was to happen next.

Unannounced, "change" showed up, like a nameless, faceless gang of angry, mad marauders—suddenly, alarmingly and unexpectedly invading every space where you live, work, play, attend school, and have your morning cup of coffee. It was September 11, 2001.

MY 9/11 EXPERIENCE

Here I am. My "diving moment" has arrived. I'm at the MC Exchange, Trinity and Rector Streets, Manhattan, New York City. It's 9:10 a.m.

I'm afraid I will never see my family, friends or work associates again. I'm concerned about my husband who is at home in our apartment in Greenwich Village. He must be frantic. No doubt he's trying to figure out if I'm ok. He's probably watching the news and seeing the Tower on fire. He knows that I was on my way to work and that my subway would stop in the WTC Concourse. I hope he's not going to try to come downtown and find me. That is not a good idea. As a matter of fact, it's a very bad idea. My cell phone isn't working and neither is anyone else's. Wait a minute. There's a phone here in the bar. Let me see if I can use it to reach him. There's a long line; but that's ok. People are trying to get in touch with their husbands, wives, and parents. Some of them have just walked down many flights of stairs in the Trade Center and their relatives are going to be sick with worry. There's a pregnant woman and her companion. They look anxious. She's afraid her mother is going to have stroke if she doesn't learn soon that her daughter is ok. It's my turn now to use the phone. I'm going to call a friend of mine who is located in close proximity to our apartment. Worse case scenario, she can run over and tell Don I'm ok and to stay where he is.

Me: Hello Carter? Call Don. Tell him I'm ok. I'm in a bar downtown. Yes, I'm safe. Honest. I don't want Don to come downtown. Tell him to stay where he is. Not to leave the apartment. Stay there. Please.
Friend: Ok. I'll tell him.
Me: The phones aren't working well. Yours is the only exchange I can reach. All of the other area codes are out. Do you mind if I call you from time to time?
Friend: Ok, that's fine. I'm on the other line with a friend in London. He said that people are jumping out of the Tower.
Me: Oh my God. Can you call Sharon? I keep calling the office but I'm not getting an answer. Find out if everyone is ok in the office.

I'm really frightened. I've never experienced anything like this before. This is different. How did I end up like this? Why didn't I get off the train at a station stop further away from here? Now it's too late. Don is going to be mad as hell that I did such a stupid, stupid thing. I could have gotten off in Brooklyn or some place far away from here. This is bad. God, why did I do this? And what am I doing holding onto this briefcase?

10:05 a.m.

Oh my God, that was so frightening. I thought the entire roof of this bar was going to cave. What happened out there? What were all of those screams about? It sounded as though the screaming was coming from high up over our heads. How is that possible? There's nothing but sky above this building. What was that? And the noise! I though we'd all be suffocated or squashed down by the roof of this place. I swear I thought I saw a bright white light—like an old-fashioned bulb going off in the dark. Something really bad is happening out there. I had a really bad feeling the moment this all started. Can't see out of the windows—it's pitch black outside. I've never seen such blackness like this. Smoke is everywhere—thick, really thick and dark—completely dense. Will we be entombed? What are we going to do? Did some kind of bomb go off?

10:10 a.m.

Wow, the lights are back on. Better find water, food, shelter. Where will we go? Should we stay here? Try to leave? No, it's too dark outside. The air is so thick. There's a man banging on the door. No one wants to let him in. I can hardly see his face. He's covered in so much debris. God, this is awful.

Me: What happened?

Man: Another plane hit. It's in the street.

Everyone is calm here. There was a moment of panic when we heard the screams outside. But when the ground started to shake and the blast went off, everyone stood very calmly and quietly in their places. I tried to find an arch to stand under. That's what you do when you're in an earthquake. What do you call this? Thank God, I had that scotch a bit ago. And I can sure use a cigarette. I'm not ready to die. I really don't want to die like this.

10:35 a.m.

I can't take much more of this. I'm glad I was in the basement for that last one. But the smoke is filling up this place fast. And it's so dark out there again. I can hardly believe it. Someone found a radio. There is a plane headed for Pennsylvania. I hope my son is ok. Could this be happening everywhere?

12:35 p.m.

I'm going to check-in with Carter again.

Me: Do you have a map?

Friend: Yes, why?

Me: I don't know where we are.

Friend: Oh.

Me: What is below the WTC? I can't figure out where I am. We can't see outside. It's very dark. I don't know where we'll go if we have to leave here.

Should we stay or go? People are asking me. I'm not sure yet. I think we should stay here awhile. I've been telling people that I've had survival training and they believe me even though it was only classroom training. It's ok. It's having a calming effect. It's not safe out there. Besides, where would we go?

1:05 p.m.

It's getting light outside. People are walking down the street with their faces covered with jackets and handkerchiefs. There's debris strewn all over the sidewalks and street. It's a mess. Looks like a nuclear winter. A few hours ago there were fire trucks heading toward the WTC. The firemen looked so resolute, calm, and accepting of their circumstances. Now there are no cars. The only movement is people making their way down the street. They look completely dazed. Their faces are beet red. A guy with a white tee shirt wrapped around his head and face is handing out wet towels and water. That's strange. There's a guy taking a bagel out of the abandoned stand over there. What a time to eat.

1:32 p.m.

It's clearing up outside. It's still foggy but at least we can see. We need to do something though. I don't think we can stay here much longer. But I don't know what is left out there. What has happened to the city? Do I still have an apartment to go home to? Is the city still standing?

1:45 p.m.

People keep asking me what we should do. I'm going outside. Have to. We need information.

2:00 p.m.

I'm outside but I'm not looking to my left toward whatever it is that hit us. Three men, very tall and muscular are walking down the street. I don't know if they are policemen or not. They have identification badges around their necks and appear to be wearing construction worker clothes.

Me: Excuse me sir—you have to come into the bar with me. There are people inside who don't know what to do. We want to know where we should go. What is safe?
Me: What should we do, should we leave here?
Men: Well, you better leave here. Tower 7 is coming down.
Me: Ok, let's get out of here everybody.
Me: Everybody! Buddy up and douse your jackets with water. Cover your nose and mouth with whatever you can find to protect yourself from that stuff out there. But let's just get out of here and head east.

(Should I leave the briefcase behind?)

4:00 p.m.

I'm home now. It was amazing. As we got a few blocks away from the bar, the sun was shining, the sky was blue and there were thousands of people on the streets and sidewalks. I remarked to my companions that it was as though we had just come off the set of an urban warfare movie. People were still frightened though. As people walked briskly down the streets, they said, "Try to stay away from the buildings, you never know when another one will be hit or come down."

There's the briefcase with the dust still inside.

As I think back over the experience of the day, I'd never been more terrified in my life. I think I sensed the scope of the danger we were in. Mostly, it was how unpredictable it all was. I remember as I watched the small TV screen that I couldn't believe this was how my life was going to end. How was this possible? I kept staring at my briefcase. I asked myself over and over, what use were the papers in this case? What was it that I had been doing with my life that was so significant? By the time I left the bar that black briefcase came to represent all that was not right with my life. At one point I left it on the end of the bar. I stared at it and thought to myself, "What value does it have now? If I get out of this alive, I should just leave it behind." But I didn't. It took awhile for me to let go of that part of my life. Eventually I did walk away from the briefcase but it wasn't until four years later. What I did take away with me that was of lasting value were the cherished memories of the people I met and with whom I shared a life altering experience. I may never see them again but they are a part of my consciousness. Those strangers became friends, if even for a short period of time. We kept each other strong and encouraged each other that we'd survive.

The MC Exchange no longer exists, another casualty of the skyrocketing Manhattan real estate boom. But for the first few years we visited that small restaurant every anniversary of 9/11. The first time we were permitted to return to Wall Street, I walked around the barricades and looked into the boarded up windows of the bar. The place looked so small to me. When it reopened I had lunch there. It was difficult. I saw James and the other people who worked there. They recognized me immediately. I felt like I was returning home—a familiar place.

What I hadn't anticipated was the mental, emotional and psychological aspects of my experience. I didn't have a strong set of coping skills. Months later I continued to suffer with enormous anxiety. I felt walled off and imprisoned—alienated from my surroundings.

Eventually, I found people in the city who were in the same dilemma. They also felt uprooted from the familiar and distant from others. We shared our stories and, little by little, we got back to our routines. We could once again feel that we had some control over our lives.

Lurking though, in the back of my mind, was a nagging question. What had caused me to feel so far estranged from my family, friends and community? This was not the first time I experienced such emotional distance. But this was different—it was prolonged and intense with no end in sight. I sensed that something needed to be addressed and would not easily be swept away or ignored.

At my son's suggestion, I searched back to my roots and to the values, beliefs and philosophy of the Italian culture. What could I find that would help me make some sense of who I was and how I became the person I am?

ALWAYS BEING PREPARED

Unlike my father, a World War II veteran, who knew his enemy, had weapons of combat, and was trained psychologically and emotionally for battle, my sole defense as a bystander in a significantly smaller war was the solid foundation he had provided me as I was growing up.

The moment had arrived when I'd put to good use those things that up until my "diving moment" arrived, I hadn't needed. I'd hold onto those lessons as my lifeline during five dark, tense hours spent seeking shelter in a small bar in lower Manhattan on 9/11. I had an experienced teacher. My father was an army veteran, a Military Policeman, fire chief and Director of Security and Safety for a naval air installation. He was a trained and experienced teacher responsible for the safety of many lives. Intentionally or not, he had taught me through word and deed how to survive worst case scenarios.

> "Pay attention".
> "Prepare for the worst."
> "Stay calm".
> "Have enough water".
> "Protect your eyes and head".
> "Always have enough money for a phone call".
> "Stay where you are if you are uncertain of the situation until you get more information".
> "Smell for smoke".

When I was a teen-ager, my father wanted me to join the armed services so that I'd learn similar disciplines as he had. But being a child of the 1960s and a "peace and love" kind of kid, I resisted the temptation to please him and his desire to see me in a "navy wave" uniform. Instead, I wore the tie-died short dresses, long hair and beads of the hippie generation.

Nevertheless, I adopted my father's cautious approach to life. I still have a piece of paper to which he carefully taped a coin in case I needed to make an emergency phone call. At best, it's a piece of nostalgia that makes me chuckle and think of my Dad. My father had given me a mind-set and survival skills that were meant to instill a sense of responsibility in me. And, I suspect, to ultimately provide him with peace of mind as I traveled through life.

During my growing up years my father carefully took into consideration all of the ways in which I might "lose control" or would need to "maintain control". Carmen would sit me down at the dining room table and teach me what he thought I was ready to learn. On one of those occasions he taught me how to safely and responsibly drink alcoholic beverages. Very systematically and conscientiously, he took the bottle of "good" twelve year old blended scotch out of the liquor cabinet. Our lesson began. He poured a shot and told me to toss it back. As I slugged it down my throat, he said I'd know what it would feel like when the liquor first hit my brain. With the second and third shot, I'd learn what my limitations were and reduce the likelihood of anyone trying to get me intoxicated. That was only one of many such lessons my father imparted to me. He taught me how to deal with car breakdowns in the middle of the night while stranded on a deserted road. "Just in case" I needed it, I had my coin on the blue note paper neatly placed in the glove compartment along with the army issue flashlight, army blanket, bottled water and Swiss knife. The first-aid kit was in the trunk—complete with butterfly band-aids, mercurochrome, smelling salts, and the instructions for conducting mouth-to-mouth resuscitation. There were other lessons to learn.

On Sundays, as we ate our family dinners of spaghetti and meatballs, Carmen engaged me in verbal combat. We debated political, moral and ethical issues until I was close to tears. He was encouraging me to understand my beliefs and develop my ability to clearly articulate my ideas and values. For instances of actual physical threat, he taught me how to hold a set of keys between the digits of my fingers—in case I had to defend myself against the aggressive acts of others. Helping people in times of need was high on my father's list of "doing the right things" along with self-defense and safety, double locking doors and making sure the fire extinguisher was in good working condition.

A DAUGHTER LEARNS

My father had been raised in a very traditional Italian family where men were supposed to be strong, fearless and uncompromising. Women weren't expected to complain but to provide a proper household for their men, children and in many cases their mothers and in-laws. This meant three meals on the table every day; everything cooked fresh—bought that day in the local markets and served on the table by 5:30 p.m. The men, for the most part blue-collar workers, left for work in the still-dark morning hours and were home by 5:00 p.m. The children, well-scrubbed and with homework complete, were attended to by the newly acquired TV that was broadcasting their favorite daytime shows. Meanwhile, every ounce of floor had been mopped and scrubbed. In many cases, plastic covered the newly purchased couches. Dad's footstool was placed in front of his favorite chair, awaiting his arrival back home that evening.

The coffee—fresh and hot off the stove—was ready to be served to a neighbor or relative stopping by for a little biscotti and espresso. Being prepared and ready for any eventuality was important. Responsibility for one's own family was essential and expected. It wasn't uncommon to have grandmom and grandpop moved to a spot in the living room when they were no longer able to care for themselves. Bedridden, grandmom became the focal point of the household once again after years of having to share attention with a grown daughter or daughter-in-law. She was firmly enshrined in her command-control center from where she could judge the quality of the Sunday gravy, the readiness of the pasta, and the behavior of the grandchildren.

This was the Italian household, everything ordered and in its place—so too, one's emotions. Not to be confused with the outsiders' interpretation of the emotional nature of the Italian. I believe that "inside", at the gut level, Italians have nerves of steel, the determination of the bull, and the expressive nature of a volcano—sometimes dormant, sometimes erupting.

To the traditional Italian, to be vulnerable is to be seen as weak. This is not respected and can also be dangerous. Italians don't like surprises and the more weakness shown, the more susceptible to the attacks of others. Respect was and still is accorded to those who are perceived to be in control and strong-minded. Italian men don't like to exhibit weaknesses, especially with their daughters. Fathers want and need to be strong and protective. Looking back, I can understand how difficult it would have been for Carmen to have told the stories of his war experiences, expressing his emotions, and being vulnerable with his family.

This was the background and the culture in which my father lived, breathed and died.

As I've come to know and appreciate many years later, to share sensitive feelings with others you need to be with people with whom you feel comfortable and can trust on an emotional level. You don't know how you are going to react once you begin expressing yourself. I believe we have a natural fear of losing control. And maybe this is the correct response when in survival mode. But, with whom and where does a person turn when they are surrounded by people and in a time and place when "being in control" is never breached or compromised? I can imagine my father trying to express himself to my grandmother and her looking at him with a thoughtful and concerned look on her face. Over half a century later, even in our newly embraced American culture, we can barely stand to see vulnerability in our leaders. We demand they portray courage, firmness and control in the face of adversity and crisis.

My father encouraged me to be a leader and not a follower. In that regard, as I grew up, I was expected to be "strong" for myself and others. I'm certain that "being in control" was a core value and, as I later learned; there is a price to pay for adhering to those standards and ways of behaving.

Knowing what I know now and with the benefit of hindsight, I might share with my father my lessons learned in this regard. He was the person who consciously and deliberately raised me within a strict code of conduct and morality. Given that he wasn't alive when my "diving moment" arrived, I have no way to communicate with him what I felt and lived. But I do have a strong enough connection with him, over twenty years after his death, that I am able to express myself to him as though he were here today standing in front of me—frozen in time.

Dear Dad:

It seems such a long time ago that I walked out of the MC Exchange at 2:00 p.m. on the afternoon of September 11, 2001. I left that experience ignorant and unable to comprehend the extent of the trauma and what it would cause in my life. When I reflect back, I am amazed at my own ability to hide such deep emotion from myself—the terror, confusion, fear, anger and yes, even shame. How do you recognize yourself when the things you took for granted are taken away so quickly?

What I've come to understand and appreciate is that expressing feelings to trusting people is both a public act and a responsibility. It is cleansing, healing and critical to our own growth and to those around us, including our families and communities.

Those "diving moments" and all the emotions that comprise them need to be integrated into the fabric of our lives—no matter how big or small, long or short in duration. Otherwise, they tend to hide in the shadows and dark corners of our individual and collective psyches.

The danger is that we can become trapped in a near constant state of anxiety, afraid of being caught off guard in a weak moment, unprepared to deal with the feelings we have grown to fear and loathe. In many ways, those feelings become larger than life itself and require a great deal of energy to keep safely locked away and out of sight.

We avoid, put aside, and distract ourselves with the lie that it's better to ignore what we don't want to acknowledge than to bring the unspoken out into the open. Those feelings might get the best of us and we could lose control. Worse yet, we could look weak in the eyes of others who would otherwise respect us if we were to have a better handle on ourselves. And most terrifying of all, we might see our own weaknesses mirrored back to us.

I wonder, as I sit here and write this letter, what happens to us when we don't adequately address our fears and unwanted emotions? Do we pay a price with lost vitality and the ability to lead real and authentic lives? I've come to believe we must deal with these things as though our life depended on it. In the end, denial does not serve us well—as human history will strongly attest. And as I learned, this tenacious need for control and subsequent inability to express feelings in an emotionally healthy way did not serve you or me very well.

I was there to witness what it had done to you but I had no way to know the cause or to learn how to avoid your folly for myself. Ultimately you suffered the consequences of your pride and your silence. It ate at you like a cancer, slowly killing you. In addition, new attacks rushed in close behind but they left no outward marks, at least not at first. The physical wounds you suffered during your war healed but not the psychic ones. They remained open, never having the opportunity to heal. What needs healing doesn't quietly go away but eventually affects every one of us where life is being denied acknowledgement.

Finally, it all caught up with you. The degenerating discs in your back forced you into early retirement and debilitated you. Once again, you tried hiding your condition from your superior officers until finally they discovered that on some days you could barely stand or walk straight. You bragged about this to me. I remember this story well.

When you were no longer able to work, you spent considerable time in the town library. That's when you found the books and the words that opened up a whole new world of thinking. You told me about the concepts that started to resonate for both of us—being vulnerable, compassionate and open to "possibility". How ironic that you gained these insights but didn't have much time to live them. Forever being the teacher, you did point out how these traits were missing in me. I think that in the fifth decade of my life, I am coming to terms with and understanding the softer side of myself.

Luckily for me, I met a special woman at a social event in Manhattan, shortly after 9/11. A stranger until the evening I met her, she engaged me in telling my story. This was not unusual and still isn't for people in New York City to share where they were when the planes crashed into the Towers or when the buildings collapsed. Debra provided me with a different kind of listening. Maybe I was ready to be heard, to be "witnessed". I don't know and I don't think it really matters that I understand. What I do know is that because of her openness and willingness to hear my story without judgment or advice, I was able to feel joy in being alive.

It's been tough Dad, learning these lessons. As I said before, I consider myself lucky. I'm getting to live what I learned and to share the best of you and me with my son.

Love from your daughter,
Jo

Not having the benefit of a response from Carmen, I can only surmise that this letter would receive his customary quiet smile and a nod of the head. On the other hand, the letter may have remained unsent, even if he were alive today.

A YOUNG MAN BEGINS A LIFE

My father, Private Carmen J. Pagano, landed in Oran, North Africa having arrived on what has been described as a "formidable convoy of troop ships." It was June 8, 1943, and the soldiers of the 45th Thunderbird Division were preparing to participate in the launch of an offensive attack—the invasion of Sicily—one of the most important operations in the war against Germany and their Italian allies. This began Carmen's involvement in the deadliest conflict in the history of humankind.

He journeyed through Italy, France, Austria and finally into Munich, Germany. Two years later, Corporal Pagano, as a member of the Military Police Platoon, stood at the gates of hell, participating in the liberation of 32,000 inmates at Dachau, the first Nazi extermination camp opened on March 23, 1933.

An Italian by birth, he had marched across two continents, and fought in various battles and campaigns to win a war for America. It was World War II and millions of people had been annihilated. By the time the 45th marched in the memorial ceremonies in Munich at the end of the war, they had logged 511 days in combat. He had collected more than enough service points to earn him his discharge. The war ended and he came home anyway—wiser, stronger, tougher, and angrier—back to the world of family, friends and the demands of building a life.

Without benefit of any real-time communications such as cell phones or email, the soldiers of World War II didn't have contact with their families for greatly extended periods of time. When Carmen returned home he was not the same man. But no one could have known that, not even him. Everything must have looked a lot smaller than he had remembered. His world had been vastly different than that of the people back home. Neither side had any frame of reference for what the other had been through.

Just two years earlier, Carmen, a twenty year old kid living in a small row house in South Philadelphia, Pennsylvania, announced to his mother that he had signed up to join the military. He walked into the kitchen where she was standing at the stove cooking pasta. He placed his square flat hands firmly on her shoulders, turned her toward him and looked her directly in the eyes. He said, "Mom, I joined the army." As simple and straight-forward as that—he offered her no further explanation. As far as my father's older brother recollects, Carmen pronounced his decision with the enthusiasm of someone who had recently learned that a long lost and forgotten relative had left him a small inheritance. My uncle still gets a big smile on his face when he recalls his younger brother's excitement.

Carmen was a handsome young man—short in stature, yet big in guts. He had thick black hair, a squared off chin, and his hazel eyes had as direct a gaze as you could get. His lips curled up naturally at the edges—there wasn't a mean bone in his body. Arriving home after the war, he carried back to his mother and waiting sweet heart a Purple Heart, Good Conduct Medal, European African Middle Eastern Service Medal with 6 bronze stars and one arrowhead. He also brought home something he could have done without—shrapnel in his head and upper back suffered while participating in a battle at Venafro, Italy—a town situated not too far from his place of birth, Salerno. He also brought home a host of memories, rarely if ever shared.

Much in a man's life is about keeping score—the number of wins and losses etched in memory over time like a bookie's "take" for the night—tallied and reminisced at the appropriate moments. By all accounts, Carmen had his share of gains and losses. During his tour of duty in World War II, his Division never won the accolades of D-Day but they were instrumental in gaining an advantage over the Germans at Anzio, Italy—one of the decisive battles of World War II. To me, that event represents a significant metaphor for his life.

Over the course of the next thirty-five years, he put every ounce of his energy toward fulfilling his version of the American dream. He never quite "made it", at least not in his eyes and not to the degree that he had hoped. His was not the bigger battle to win—he never won his D-Day—but the lesser known, smaller, every day battles of surviving and providing for his family. My father was a fireman, and in today's world, a hero. In the 1950s, 1960s, and 1970s he was simply a blue-collar worker. He never completed high school, yet rose to the position of fire chief as a civilian employee of the Department of the Navy.

Carmen was respected by his men and his superior officers. At one point in his career, he lost his position as chief, due to various government installation shutdowns and assumed the role of Fire Safety Inspector. Nevertheless, he doggedly persisted in regaining his earlier role and, after several years of effort, he once again became a fire chief. Over those years, whether or not he officially held the title, everyone he worked with referred to him as "chief". His frustration continued, however, as he worked hard to attain a higher pay status, and in those efforts he didn't meet his goal. He wrote and submitted report after report to his superior officers explaining why he was qualified for that next level. He kept these papers in a neat file which I have in my possession. It was a big disappointment to him that he couldn't get the promotion and earn more money. He was quite vocal about it to me.

In his fifth decade of life, he traveled long distances to and from his work to keep his family financially solvent. I'm sure there were many worrisome times for him. His car was like a third child in the family. He babied "Betsy"—taking care of her, tending to her, ensuring that her engine would start on cold, snowy mornings. Every night during the long winter months, he'd be in the garage tinkering and getting her ready for the next morning. The battery was safely in place to ensure she'd start up and carry him to his work destination. Friends would tease him about the car. I found a letter written to him by a friend who was serving in Viet Nam at the time. His buddy asked, "How's the wife and family, chief? Oh and how's the car, ha ha!"

Among the many dreams my father had for his family, the one of me "being a debutante" was completely outlandish, given our social and economic status but reveal his high aspirations. Carmen didn't dream "small"; he knew what "climbing the social ladder" meant but didn't have the wherewithal to reach it. At the very least, he painted the picture and held it up for me to see for myself. Is this what aspiring immigrant fathers do for their children? Although he carefully guarded the spending of every penny, he taught me that it's better to own "one good thing" than a "lot of junk". He frowned on gaudiness and loudness of any kind. That is not to say that Carmen didn't have moments when he lost the tight grip he had over his carefully controlled emotions.

Occasionally, I had glimpses of his temper and as a result, I'm glad he rarely acted on those feelings. He was a strong, tough guy who you wouldn't want to underestimate during a conflict. He'd take you by surprise. You would be fooled into thinking his quiet demeanor was a possible show of weakness. You didn't dare this man. He was the kind of guy who, as a teenager, played Russian roulette with live rounds of ammo and didn't blink an eye. His motto was, "If there's something you're afraid of—conquer it—by doing it despite your fears". He was protective of me yet he wanted me to be strong. He encouraged my willfulness and once remarked, "If there's anything I can say about you, it's that you can't be bought". Coming from him, that was no small complement. He knew that, like him, once I had made a decision, there was no turning back. No amount of bribery, reward or punishment would deter me from the course of action I had decided upon. It was that kind of behavior he admired in a person and I respected him for it.

There was no doubt, however, that he had a love of the good things life had to offer. By his way of thinking, you just had to figure out how to get them and what the trade-offs were going to be in return. He was in the habit of researching the best wines, scotches and champagnes he could afford to buy or if he couldn't, he'd wait and save enough money so he could get what he wanted.

Wherever I lived, he identified the "desirable" neighborhoods and schools where his grandson should grow up and be educated. He wasn't shy about telling you his opinions. He spent a lot of time thinking and planning ahead and when he was ready, he shared the outcome of those day dreams.

I'm certain he influenced my choices and my desire to enjoy the best in life. He often referred to people who had higher social status than himself as "big" and openly encouraged me to seek out those opportunities that would get me closer to that world. From how I looked, dressed, ate and behaved—my father pointed out what the "big people do"—and that should be my benchmark in creating my life.

He wanted me to live in an upper middle-class neighborhood, wear fine clothes, have the "right" friends and marry a man who was upwardly mobile. He was happy to learn that I was capable of doing all of those things as evidenced by the company I kept, the places I worked, how I entertained and how I dressed.

A few years after his death, I had acquired the Mercedes, the nice house in the good suburban neighborhood, the clothes, a family business—all the trimmings and trappings that he dreamed for me. By the time I was forty years old, I earned more money than he ever did, had a bigger house, a better car and an education. I wasn't a debutante but I rubbed shoulders and was friends with the "big" people he admired, emulated and respected.

It came as no surprise for me to learn that when my father was growing up he was ashamed of being an Italian immigrant. When he signed up for World War II he stated on his application papers that he was a United States citizen. Fortunately for him, the army draft board, needing able-bodied men, registered him as an alien and inducted him into the army. A few months later he was naturalized and made a citizen.

It's interesting to me that neither of his parents had been naturalized and Carmen lived in America for twenty years without his citizenship. It wasn't until my grandmother was fifty years old that she signed a "Declaration of Intent" and received an alien registration card. After the war, when Carmen was applying for a firefighter position, he stated once again he was born in Philadelphia. Subsequently, he explained in a letter to the Labor Board,

---

15 October 1945
"The reason why I stated that I was born in Phila., Pa. in my Guard and Fire-fighter applications is because I was ashamed of the fact that I was born in

Italy. I came to the United States when I was thirteen months old. I considered myself as having been born in Philadelphia, Pa., because I resided there practically all my life. In all future Civil Service papers that I may execute, I positively will give full and complete information about my place of birth, namely Italy."

My father had very strong beliefs about America, freedom, democracy and that dream called "opportunity". Although he was only thirteen months old when he came to this country he had the "face and the spirit" of America's immigrants. His battle, I believe, was an inner one—he literally fought to belong and to earn his stripes. As I was growing up, he spoke passionately about "this country". I'm not certain why or how he came to have such strong beliefs. I can only surmise. He had the strongest conscience of anyone I know or probably ever will. His brothers and sister always spoke of him as "different". He possessed a distinct set of expectations and values for his life but in his youth had limited opportunity for expressing himself.

I don't know who or where he drew from as far as his role models were concerned. Maybe he had an uncle, friend, war or cinema hero that he admired. How did he decide what kind of life he wanted for himself and ultimately for his family? On the surface, he was a serious, intense, honest, and loyal kid—completely devoted to his mother. After he married and started a family, he didn't take his role as father any less seriously. He applied the same passion, commitment, diligence and values that he had espoused as a young man toward ingraining those ideals in his children.

Maybe there is something to be said for the influence of a country's values, especially America in the 1930s and 1940s. Life, liberty and the pursuit of happiness—ideals, hope and dreams he never abandoned to the end of his life.

Looking Back to Go Forward

○ ○

"It's often said that much of what we call a "life" is actually lived in reverse. While we're living our daily lives, there is little time for reflection on where we came from or how we arrived at a point in time with the ideas, beliefs and attitudes that we have.

Left unexamined, much of the life we actually live is "fixed", slowly becoming the seeds for our own fall from original grace. Lifeless, lacking in curiosity, no longer able to learn—becoming dead to ourselves and others—we find ourselves wandering through a landscape that no longer makes any sense. Mostly, we don't know that there is a difference. Expelled from Eden, we experience the death of expectation, desire, anticipation, hunger, and dissatisfaction. In its place numbness, false faces, masks, and insincerity fill the gap. The only recourse is to fix, hide and paint over the parts of ourselves that we no longer want to see. To recover ourselves, we must look back to go forward."

THE BETSY STORY

Fortunately for me, I had a captive audience early on in my story telling career. It began every day at 7 o'clock in the morning as my school friends and I dutifully marched off to school and back home again. A story I've shared often with other audiences of friends and acquaintances is about me and a girl named Betsy.

Betsy lived across the street from our family in an Italian neighborhood in West Philadelphia. I was five years old and lived in a semi-detached row house on Robinson Street. There was a small front porch, lots of concrete sidewalk and a driveway with a detached garage. Since everything was situated close together it was hard to escape the watchful eye of neighbors who were always in each others business—especially children. And so it was for me. Nearly every time I stepped out of the house to play, this girl Betsy would appear, threatening and sometimes hitting me. I'd run back into the house crying to my mother, afraid to return outside.

One day my mother lost her patience and sent me back outside to learn how to defend myself or else face the wrath of her anger. One way or another, I was going to have to deal with the situation—face my mother or face Betsy. I had to confront my fears and it was upsetting.

Recently, I reflected on what I might say to Betsy if I were to talk with her today. Might things have ended differently between us? If so, would it have sent me on another path or course of action in my life? There are many unanswered questions, and one can only speculate as one looks back to go forward.

Dear Betsy:

I've told our story so many times. To this day, you are and will forever remain five years old. You may not be alive today. Or you may have many children of your own and will have forgotten the incident that happened between us over fifty years ago. What would I say to you now if you and I were to meet each other as adults?

I'd probably discuss with you whether or not we could have settled our differences peacefully. And what was with you anyway that you had to hit me every time you saw me? Did I offend you in some way? Come on now! I was small, defenseless and you were bigger than me. What set you off? What did I do that provoked you to want to hit me? Did I look at you in some weird way? Did I make fun of you? I honestly don't remember. If I did, I'm sorry; I hope you can forgive me for that, if it happened.

In my mind, you were and still are a bully—a girl who was big for her age, who probably didn't have many friends. Maybe you wanted attention and so you hit me. Maybe I ignored you. I don't know—won't ever know, of that I'm sure. Whatever happened between us is lost forever—except for what happened afterwards. My hitting you, that is. You see, I really didn't want to hurt you. But I was more afraid of my mother than I was of you. So the one last time you hit me, I hit you back—worse than you ever hit me. You cried and ran to tell your mother. Your mother called my mother, but I didn't get punished. My mother was pleased. She didn't care about you. I hope your mother cared, though. Maybe that was your problem. I wish it weren't so, for your sake. As I recall, you and I never played together or spoke after that incident.

I'm sorry Betsy. If I had to do it all over again, I'd probably try to find some other way to reconcile our differences. That way, I wouldn't have hurt my brother or my best friend Bobby when they made me angry. You see, you taught me how to fight and I'm not proud of that. I hope you aren't, either.

My encounter with Betsy broke new ground for me. She became a part of the repertoire of my life story. Not only did it impact subsequent relationships but also my view of motherhood and philosophy of life which, through my only child's growing up years, I struggled to change my behavior. Whether or not my mother had any forethought about what she did or how she treated a seemingly innocent situation, her reaction to my distress and her solution to my problem left its mark. So begins the many stories that comprise my relationship with my mother.

MY MOTHER

Our family moved to the suburbs of Philadelphia just in time for me to begin first grade in St. Lawrence's parish, a Catholic school not too far from our house. I walked to the bus stop with my mother on the first day of school wearing a brand new maroon one-piece uniform with a white rounded-collar blouse, complete with white bobby socks and black and white newly polished saddle shoes. I managed to walk several yards behind my mother. I don't recall having the least bit of fear of the unknown world I was about to enter, having successfully dealt with my first bully, Betsy. I was ready.

We were in a new neighborhood in the suburbs, miles from the city where the rest of our extended family lived—away from grandparents, aunts, uncles and cousins. I had never attended Kindergarten or any other social event, outside of the circle of our small, close-knit Italian family. No, I was not afraid; instead, I was embarrassed by my mothers' big black coat, her jet-black hair, and dark skin—the kerchief on her head. I had already made the discovery that no one else in our new neighborhood looked like her. It's interesting how quickly children discover these things. It's as if you have this special radar that sounds an alarm when anything your parents do or say is likely to embarrass you. Parents are embarrassing to children no matter what they do.

I was soon to find out, though, that others would feel the same about me. I did not know that I had entered a new world where I was the outsider—even though we all wore the same uniforms. From West and South Philadelphia to the lily white suburbs, Italians were not welcomed with open arms, especially dark haired, dark skinned girls with thick Philadelphia accents, carrying lunch boxes filled with sandwiches consisting of sharp cheese and strong smelling salami.

The mother of a good friend of mine who also lived in that same suburban neighborhood, remarked to me years later that it was "tough for you growing up" there. She said "Your kind was not accepted; you had it hard."

Other close friends of the family who had lived in the suburbs years before we arrived attempted to educate me into the ways of this new environment. My mother's best friend gave me a book to help me with my grooming—there were ideas and activities on how to walk, talk, dress and act like a lady. There were strict rules for proper dressing in the 1950s and early 1960s—seamed stockings, girdles, long-line bras, Chesterfield coats, starched collars, hair bows, hats and white gloves—all requiring careful attention. I kept my "good grooming" book on my bed-side table—next to my Sunday prayer book, rosary beads and eventually my Girl Scout handbook.

I didn't want to look, act or dress like my mother. I don't recall having many heart-to-heart conversations with her during my early years. I loved and valued her as a mother and was upset when she was ill or occasionally hospitalized but it was an uneasy alliance. We occupied different worlds. I never wrote her letters—unsent or otherwise. Mostly I gave her greeting cards for mother's day, Easter and her birthday.

I remember the year when my father and I failed to get her birthday cards. That was not a good day for our household. My father would ask me to mark the date on my calendar, so we wouldn't slip up and forget to buy the cards. Much like my father, my mother became more open, vulnerable, approachable and "soft" in her fifth decade of life. When she died at age sixty-two she was a different woman than the person who raised me. The woman had a hard time in life and she was filled with regrets for what didn't happen, couldn't happen and would never happen for her. So who was I to try to have it all?

Unsent Letter, 2005

Mom:

It's been a long time since we've spoken. I still have dreams about you where I haven't called or been to your house and I feel such guilt and remorse that I'm moved to weeping until I awake and remember that you are dead and long gone. The dreams haunt and are reminders of the things that were never said, shared or acknowledged. You rarely spoke about growing up or about your family. My imagination gets the best of me sometimes and I fantasize about what "might have happened" in your life that would cause you to be such an angry, unhappy and restless woman.

Despite the anger, the hitting and the yelling I don't ever remember being afraid of you except when you forced me to confront Betsy. That may have been the first and last time. I think I knew with a child's instinct that you'd never really hurt me. Or maybe I wished it to be so.

Once, however, you did almost really hurt me. I'll never forget that incident. You were angry about something and had a bad headache, not unusual for you, and you took to the bed. You'd say, "I'm going upstairs to lie down. I have a headache." And you would lie on the bed, on top of the covers, fully clothed barely taking off your shoes. Sometimes the door would be open, on other occasions it would be closed. The house was silent during these "headache" episodes. I think we knew that this was a dangerous time. The house became church-like, almost monastic—maybe we were praying or saying a novena that you'd wake up refreshed and in a good mood. During one of these occasions, I broke the silence. I don't recall what I did or attempted to do but I entered your bedroom and said or did something that was forbidden. You became enraged. From the bed, you sat up and got one of your shoes and threw it at me. The heel hit my right eye. I can still feel the impact of that heel on my eyeball. I thought I was blinded. Years after this incident, during a routine eye examination, my doctor told me that there is a significant difference between my two eyes.

Perhaps who I became as a teenager had nothing to do with rebelliousness. I was a little weird as a child. I know this bothered you. All that reading, all that curiosity about things—you'd ask me, "Why do you always have to know 'WHY' all the time?" "Stop asking me all of those questions." Maybe my feeling different had nothing to do with being Italian in a "white" neighborhood but went far deeper. And yet, your anger, ridicule and questioning never stopped me from doing what I wanted to do.

If anything, I became more determined to have my way. If I liked something, I pursued it, whether it was the clothes I wore or the music I gravitated toward. I spent hours, sometimes entire days, writing in my journal in our attic. When I first read Anne Frank I thought I had found a soul mate. That was my solace away from the sometimes chaotic nature of our house.

And yet, I don't blame or think ill or badly about you—the mother of my childhood. I understand how you could not have been any other way than whom and what you were. You had few role models. How could you have known that you were causing such pain to your family with your strictness and the other ways in which you exacted control? The world was approaching the 1960s and a time when everything was being questioned—even motherhood and womanhood itself. Maintaining a household based on the old traditions must have been very difficult and probably felt like a losing battle. Yet, with no recourse to another game plan, you just tried harder.

Do you know what I think, Mom? I think you had a feeling deep down in your soul that there was something you wanted to be or do that had been denied to you. You had a glimpse of it sometime in your girlhood. I can see it in your eyes in the pictures that were taken of you when you visited your mother's farm in Vineland during your summer's off from school. You looked so confident, so bright—you glowed with your power. You were full of your young, vital budding womanhood. Your own mother was a very strong, smart woman. She raised nine children, owned real-estate, was a bail-bonds person, sold boot-leg liquor during the prohibition years and took in boarders. She was the bread winner in the family, and a very good one at that. You never suffered during the depression and lived in a beautifully furnished three-story row house in Philadelphia. Your sisters were headstrong, willful and outspoken women. In many ways they were completely outrageous with their gaudy jewelry and bright clothes, finger nails pained bright red, and earrings dangling.

What happened to shut you down and silence you? What cut you off from your talents, goals and dreams? Why did you wear those dark clothes when you went outside the house and keep yourself so plain? Mom, let's face it. You were never happy. Not after you married my father. You said to me shortly after his death that he clipped our wings—we could never be the butterflies that we were. I'll never forget your words. "He clipped our wings so we could not fly." Mom, I think you were talking about yourself. I flew—maybe not as far as I would have liked—but I flew. You never did. Not even after Dad was gone. You stayed close to home base; never straying too far away. I urged you to create a new life for yourself. You always wanted to live in the city. When you could finally do the things you said you wanted, you had so much fear that you couldn't "fly". You never learned.

While Dad was alive, you started to venture out with your girlfriends and would go on vacation with them. You began spending more time with your sisters. But you never did the thing that remained unspent, unused, and therefore, unacknowledged. And that became your albatross. You medicated yourself with food. Even after several heart attacks you didn't change your diet. You kept eating, trying to fill yourself up; what was empty for you could never be satisfied.

In the end, you died giving up your chance to live. Your last act of submission occurred while you were waiting to have bypass surgery. The surgeon and doctors came into the hospital room and asked for your permission to postpone your operation so that a man could have his before you. They said his case was more critical than yours. I urged you to not give up your place but you said, "No, you can take him first. I'll wait. He needs this worse than I do." Several doctors, while standing over your hospital bed convinced you to "do the right thing" for this man and his family.

They were angry with me because I fought them on this decision. That is why they approached you; as sick as you were. This man had one artery that was clogged; you had over 90% of yours that were blocked. It's not difficult to do the math on this one.

You acquiesced. I was there. I know. And I let you go. You chose your ending. And in some ways I guess that is how you would have wanted it regardless of the circumstances. You controlled how you departed and I was very angry with you for leaving me in that way. But I think I understand.

I feel very sad writing this letter to you. It doesn't settle anything between us. It just opens up more questions, emotions, and anxieties. But the good thing is I don't feel remorse or guilt for anything I did or said—I hope you were finally at rest with it all during your last days and nights.

I continue to remember you every day of my life. I keep with me the memories of our last years together. We finally got to spend time together where we just sat with one another—no activities, just the two of us. It came to your being sick and in the hospital to finally get you to a place where you had time to just be yourself. No cooking, cleaning, shopping, walking, hopping the bus to the casinos or doing all of that stuff you did so you didn't have to deal with yourself or your life. I guess that's the only way you and I would have had the time and space to face each other, as two women, looking back, talking with each other about our regrets and our hopes.

During the last week of your life you said to me, "I was too hard on you when you were growing up. I expected you to be perfect."

Mom—that was the best thing you ever said to me.

Your daughter,
Jo

This letter leaves me thinking. I ask myself, "How did I come to be who I am? What did I learn that would benefit me in my life? Would I need to unlearn certain things so that I wouldn't repeat the mistakes of the past or cause harm to another because of my own ignorance or blindness?"

Most people hate questions. It's all that I have.

FIRST RELATIONSHIPS

o o o o o o o o o o o o o o o o o o o o o o o o o o o o o o o o

"There are numerous people, places and events that conspire to influence our lives. Exactly who and what they are, for the most part, remains hidden and out of view. Not until we dig around in the dustbins of the past is there some light shed on what may be still lurking—haunting us and popping up in the oddest moments. Do they become part of our dreams, encoded and encrypted in such a way that it takes considerable effort to decipher their meaning? Is any life ultimately coherent, full of meaning and purpose? Or do we invent it along the way, in the hopes that we can make some sense of our experiences?

What is a life anyway, but a pack of stories, memories, and events struggling for cohesiveness?

THE ITALIAN GIRL

Sometime in grade school I became friends with an Italian girl who had just arrived from her family's home town in Sicily. I don't recall her name but I can picture her as she was then. She was very dark-skinned, thin, awkward and gangly.

To look at her was to feel sorry for her. But not so to my classmates in the Catholic school I attended. Every chance they got, they mocked her, calling her names, making fun of her—especially when Sister Mary Joseph left the classroom.

One day, the nun had to run an errand—leaving us just long enough for mischief to occur. The taunting of the poor girl began. But that day I had had enough of my classmates' nonsense. I arose from my desk, walked over to her and put my arms around her shoulders. I glared at the boys. "You just dare me", my gaze said. At twelve years old, I was bigger and taller than most boys my age and that had its advantages. I was capable of overpowering the biggest among them and they knew it.

The Italian girl was never harassed again—at least, not in my presence. After that, her big Italian family adopted me.

From then on, many Sunday afternoons were spent at their house, eating pasta, and singing along to Italian operas.

MY FIRST FRIEND

My first real friendship came when I was in fifth grade. I was walking home from school with my big manly looking briefcase filled with books. It was one of those top loading, heavy leather cases that lawyers or school teachers carried. As I was walking along the sidewalk, I heard my name called out, "Josephine!" I turned and saw a very pretty girl. Tall, with long, smooth and perfectly groomed blond hair, she had very white teeth and a wide smile. Her clear blue eyes were quick to turn mischievous. We were standing on the sidewalk of a street not far from our grade school, in front of a house with a white picket fence.

The details are vivid to me. This girl had great posture and a spotlessly clean school uniform. She and I became best friends. She had just moved to our neighborhood and was living a block away from my house. I considered this a stroke of good luck. Having the most popular girl in the neighborhood call you "friend" can make a difference when you're not so popular yourself. There were few sororities where I was welcome as a member and she declined invitations to all of them as a result. We formed our own sorority with a great group of girls. We had many good times together—all of which I recorded detail by detail in my diaries. We ice skated in winter at the Lansdowne Ice & Coal rink, attended dances at the Highland Park Canteen and Holy Cross and hung out at Gino's, the Dairy Queen and the Drexel Hill Bowling Alley. We played our various musical instruments in the High School Orchestra, participated in concerts, listened to the Beatles, danced and talked about our favorite topic—boys.

Oftentimes, she and I would walk each other back and forth from her house to mine until the sky darkened and we knew we'd be in trouble with our mothers for not getting home on time for dinner. But we didn't care—we had many things to discuss. There was a tree in a neighbor's back yard where we liked to sit and talk. I carved our initials there inside a heart. I loved that girl—she listened and was kind and thoughtful. I don't remember what we spoke about but whatever it was I felt calm and reassured that the world was an ok place to be.

Things changed though when my friend's father died. He was an elegant man—kind, quiet, gentle, and intelligent. I think we all suffered as a result of his death. For many of us girls it was our first real loss of a significant person in our lives. My relationship with my friend shifted after that—we weren't as close as we were before her father died.

I felt the void left by our friendship but there wasn't much to do but to move on.

FLUFFY

There was another girl who I met in high school during our freshmen year. We were in the orchestra together and spent countless hours in music practice. Fluffy was a true outlier and as a result, didn't join my "group". She never was part of any sorority—a loner, she carefully chose her friends, and there weren't many. She was my first soul sister. To this day I think about her. There have been several Fluffy's in my life but she set the standard.

We never missed a Saturday night dance at Holy Cross high school. When we arrived, we'd try to get as close to the front door of the auditorium as possible so we could be the first ones to get into the dance. Once inside, there was a cool darkness. Attending an "all girl's" Catholic High School from morning until evening, five days a week, made the Holy Cross dance an activity to look forward to. We danced for hours. At the end of the night, we counted the number of new boys we met and how many asked us to dance.

Later that evening we'd dutifully record the number, names and activities in our diaries.

In between our various school and social activities, Fluffy and I had many deep philosophical discussions. We loved having pajama parties, and she and I would spend entire evenings playing with the Ouija board asking it various questions about our lives. She and I attended the World's Fair in New York in 1964 with her family.

I was entranced. It was my first trip out of the Philadelphia area. That morning, when the alarm clock rang, the Rolling Stones song, "I Can't Get No Satisfaction" played. We were ready to leave for New York and to have some adventures.

I wrote Fluffy a letter in sophomore year but never mailed it to her. It was the first time I set pen to paper to share my story with a good friend. It was also to become one of the many unsent letters to friends and family members that, along with my journals and diaries, were typically never shared.

Unsent Letter to Fluffy circa 1965

Dear Fluffy

I'm sitting here at my desk, with the radio on beside me (7:25). I guess I'll start with the beginning of my life. From what I heard, they had a hard time getting me into the world, from the first day I was on earth, I was a stubborn thing. I was a sickly little kid, too. I was very quiet and people predicted that I'd become a nun. I used to sit inside, read, play, and watch TV. I wasn't allowed away from the house very much. My first social problem was the girl next door. She was big for her age. I was small and skinny so she took advantage of me, and used to beat me up whenever I went outside. My mother quickly solved this problem by beating me every time I came in crying. You can guess what my reaction was, and it was her turn to run, crying to her mother. From that time on, I was a little bully. Every time someone (a kid, of course) would put a foot on our lawn, I'd beat them up. We moved when I was 5 years old. The first day at our new house, a little boy was sitting on our curb and the next thing you know, I ordered him from our house or else I'd beat him up. He just looked at me, and then took my hand and we took a walk. He told me I was pretty and from that time on, we were best friends. We did everything together. But don't think I didn't boss him around. One day he called me a name and I threw some sticks with thorns on them at him. I was continually bossing everybody around, as I was the only girl in the neighborhood among fifteen boys. The neighbors used to tell my mother to tame me down before it was too late. In school, I was the same until fifth grade, because I was tired of bossing everybody so I became the class clown. I started to flunk tests deliberately, to be funny. Up to this time, I had gotten 1st honors. In grade school, I never got along with boys. They used to treat me like a tomboy (which I was). I used to chase after them, even though they couldn't stand me. Then I went to the other extreme in sixth grade. I was very serious. In seventh and eighth grade I was a clown again (popular with girls and not boys). In freshmen year, boys suddenly took an interest in me and in the summer when I was fourteen years old, fifteen boys tried to break into my house. I was doing well in school and my social life was pretty good but I wasn't allowed to date. In the summer after freshmen year, I was asked out a lot but I wasn't allowed so that when sophomore year came, I rebelled and you know what happened. I was pretty close to being a hoodlum (except I didn't steal or anything like that). Due to security reasons I can't go into details about what I did. After I broke up with Rick, I started settling down a little. But from Jan. to May was one big bore, except for the sailors. The summer after sophomore year was good and now we're up to this year. I am completely reformed now. I'm not jive any longer, etc. But now I have a non-trusting complex. I don't trust anyone anymore, Fluffy. I was let down too many times and hurt by both boys and girls to trust anyone anymore. I still don't know my real self; I change my mind about things from week to week. In all my 16 years, I haven't accomplished anything or completed anything I've started. I'm mentally lazy, and I brag too much. I usually give a person the wrong impression from what I feel. I feel like I have built a shell around myself, no one can reach me and I can't reach anyone. Every time I put my faith and trust in someone, they disappoint me. Maybe, because I expect too much but I'm willing to give. I'm moody, bad temper, very sensitive, and too serious, and too silly at times. I've tried to conquer my faults but they're conquering me.

I've written the first things that came into my head. I've read it over and it doesn't make sense. But I feel a little better now.

Growing Up in the 60s

o o o o o o o o o o o o o o o o o o o o o o o o o o o o o o o o o

"Does the need for rebellion ever stop?"

KEEPING JOURNALS

I kept a diary and wrote in numerous journals throughout my life beginning in grade school and now into my adult years. Growing up I found it difficult to verbally express my thoughts and feelings to others. My consolation was writing at my small desk in a corner alcove of the attic in our house on Woodlawn Avenue. From that vantage point, I could see the tops of the trees and planes flying low as they made their descent toward the Philadelphia airport. I could hear the laughter and shouts of the children down below playing basketball, jumping rope and chasing one another around the rows of houses and clothes lines. Not loud enough to be a distraction, the noise remained a sweet, quiet hum reminding me that life was being lived. In the attic, I was surrounded by old books, paper and pencils. That was heaven to me.

Now, as I sit in my apartment in Greenwich Village, watching the planes approaching La Guardia, I can hear the purring of the motorcycles down below and the banging of the trucks as they hit the bumps and ruts in the street. I live on a street called "Broadway", and write, listen, and think, while hunched over my laptop creating new material based on my old diary and journal entries, unsent letters and newly written ones. I read and re-read the diaries from fifty years ago and am glad I kept these papers. If I hadn't, I might not believe my own stories, thinking that I may have fictionalized them to make them more interesting. I have no excuses for anything I wrote or felt. It is commentary and a reflection of the times in which I lived, the people who surrounded me and the circumstances of our lives.

In my early years, I wrote in my diary nearly every day. Usually, I recounted the events, including bits of conversations with friends and the details of our activities. Nothing was too mundane—boys met, tests taken, phone calls shared, ice skating and dances, parties attended—all were noted. People's nicknames and pet peeves, movies seen, each entry reminding me of the days, nights and the passing of years. As to be expected, things changed as I entered my teenage years. Mostly I wrote when I was depressed, unhappy or anxious especially when I began to meet and date boys.

The 1960s were an exciting, fascinating and confusing time. Everything was changing including a way of life I had lived—influenced by Old World values and attitudes—that no longer seemed to fit what was emerging. There was more freedom of expression, liberation, and rebellion against the old, the status quo and the established. We were a generation undergoing deep change and there were few, if any, anchors other than our family and church values to offer some measure of stability.

And yet, these were the very things we wanted to overthrow. When I look back over the decade of the 1960s I wonder what really changed, if anything. For me, my innate rebelliousness was fueled by the rhetoric of the time. I felt the agitation of the masses to break free from restriction although there was no vision of what might take the place of the things we didn't like or what we wanted for our new world.

Who or what was I to become if not more of the same of what came before me? My world was being rocked and there was no turning back. But where was I to turn with all of these feelings of turmoil, desire and longing for something as yet unnamed, unformed and untested? Once again, through my writing, I found an outlet for expressing my personal angst. Sometimes I had the urge to write about people who didn't exist but my pen willed them into life. I created my own heroes and anti-heroes. Mostly I observed people, usually sitting in coffee shops or dive bars in central Philadelphia. I couldn't draw so I sketched in words what I "saw" in life.

Journal Entry, circa 1960s

"Sitting on a bed, in a dingy dim lit room we see a young man, deep in thought. His expression conveys deep emotional turmoil. His dark brown hands are clutching his head as if this action could make clear his thoughts. The voices that were hushed are now rising to a crescendo. This jolts him to a sitting position and he lifts his broad frame from the bed. He listens intently to the two voices. Remorse takes possession of his handsome face making it appear aged, and then his face becomes expressionless. The only sign of action are his eyes darting from side to side as if he were trying to read the words they were saying. He hesitates for a moment and puts his hand on the doorknob but then he sullenly turns around and walks toward his bed. He starts wringing his hands in a frenzy of despair. His head slowly sinks down on his chest and once more his face becomes expressionless."

Poem, circa 1960s

He sits in a bar
Drinks his taste
Blank, empty face of a
Half-man

She sits and types
Watches the clock
Takes her break
She's a routine.

They walk fast
Shop in stores
Buy clothes for occasions
That may never come
Cook a meal
Clean the dishes
Eat and sleep
Play

Journal Entry, circa 1960s

I haven't written anything in a diary for such a long time. I miss the confidence which I had in writing. My self-expression tends to be verbal now. I always used to write everything. Now I let it out.

I saw "The Fixer" today. I wish I had some cause to fight for. All I am fighting for right now is freedom. The Freedom to do, say, feel what I want. Maybe I am just like every other teenager who feels too restricted but then again my complaints are justified. Then again there are people who are worse off. But to each individual, his own restrictions are the worst. Even though he may not have physical pain because of such restrictions or conditions which incite pain, the pain which he inflicts upon himself may be just as damaging.

Here, my whole youth is going away so fast and I am not aggressive enough to find some outlet for my energy and time. With so many suffering people here I sit on my ass, letting these things happen without lifting a finger.

Some reminders: Ask adviser about volunteer or social work. Read more. Modern dance lessons. I wish to God that He would let me see some light or some hope in man. I wish I could utilize my tremendous emotional capacity.

I wrote a piece when I was thirteen years old or thereabouts. When I read this journal entry, I have a faint recollection of sitting at my desk in my bedroom as I wrote it. I was imagining a young man, barely out of his teens, who would have the capacity to lead the youth of his day out of their anxiety and confusion. Perhaps, unknowingly I was asking for a "sign".

It was around the time John F. Kennedy was assassinated and I could see we were in bad shape but felt alone and helpless in the face of such overwhelming evidence that all was not right with the world. To this day, the journal entry remains unedited and intact with a few minor changes for coherence. I never shared this writing with anyone but had it stored in a filing bin, perhaps waiting for a time when it would make some sense.

The Beatles were barely on the horizon yet I remember that I was very much taken by the messages of their songs.

Was I asking for help? Apparently, I wasn't seeking guidance from our religious, government or educational institutions. No parents, teachers, grandparents, aunts or uncles could answer my questions or provide solace.

I wonder how much or how little has changed for our youth as they struggle with their fears, concerns, and barely conscious anxieties?

Journal Entry, circa 1960s

"By all means he'd have a message. And this message would be put into his records because records are the most listened to thing there is. I know that to be true because in some records they try to bring out a point and the record is listened to over and over and is discussed and we tell each other how we feel about it. For example, when a record comes on the radio you listen to it; if it isn't a bunch of loud noise you think about what they're saying. And sometimes you get a lesson or a moral out of it. As to what the message would say is the problem because a really good solution hasn't come up yet. But it would not be blunt and he wouldn't come rite out and say it. He would use symbolism, but in a powerful way and subtle so that most people will think they discovered it for themselves. It would make them feel better and it would bring a sense of achievement. Most teens rebel against someone coming right out and saying this is what you should do and this is what you shouldn't do. Another way the message would be brought out is in books because a lot of teens are reading now. But again, written in such a way as to put out the message, yet not truly revealing it. Generally speaking adults might try to understand him but couldn't fully because it's not their problems and the books or records are not written for them. I don't mean it to sound that we'd have him all for ourselves but why should adults have to fully understand him. If they can't understand us how could they understand him? But we would need their approval because first of all if they didn't approve, then some teens would only listen to him, out of rebellion and then the other half who respect their parents' judgment, wouldn't bother with him. But then we have the middle group who respect their own judgment and then form their own opinion without any rebellion pushing them or doubt puzzling them. So I conclude that to make matters better adults would generally approve of him. This boy would make no demands on us because we would follow him because we respected him and yet he wouldn't be making any laws. He would have to be forceful though and vigorous. He would change our way of living because that's why we need him. To help us lead better, fuller lives. Because there are many teens who are in bad shape.

First of all it would have to be a teenager himself because he alone can under-stand the problems facing his generation. It couldn't be an adult because then it would put us on our guard. We'd be thinking, "What are they trying to trap us into now?" This doesn't include all teens though because many of them realize that adults have more experience and are the best people to turn to for advice. So to compromise between the two, the person would have to be between 23 and 26. I say older than 21 because a 21 year old is just experiencing more freedom and is not so experienced as an older person as to handle all this freedom. I think a boy would be best suited because boys aren't about to take to a girl leading them. And girls would also prefer a boy I imagine. The boy would have traveled a bit, to be more experienced, know different people and places. He'd be a singer because they travel and when they put out a record, people listen to it, if they like it they buy more records and then read up on this person to find out about his personality and life. He should have a lot of talent and be very humorous because no one wants to listen to a lot of monotonous talk. And of course he'd be good looking because generally people only see the outer part of a person and then they judge whether they like him or not. He'd be different. By different I mean he wouldn't be just a common ordinary boy. He'd have his own ideas; he wouldn't be a carbon copy of the long hair, tight pants majority of boys. I'm not trying to portray a slick looking singer but someone whom everyone can look up to. I don't know any person existing now who is like this but this would be my image of a person who could rise above everyone, make himself known by modest means and come to our aid.

Claiming My Power

○ ○

"Let the past speak for itself."

WHAT'S HIS NAME

Shortly after I graduated from High School my mother said to me, "So, when are you going to get married?" There wasn't much analysis or thought given to the matter. It was more about choosing someone, getting married, buying a house and starting a family. It was the thing to do—for better or for worse.

I wrote a small unsent poem to my high school boyfriend and soon to be future husband.

> I cannot wish you harm and yet
> Sometimes I wish that you might
> Have some grief
> a very little grief
> So you would
> come into my arms
> and cry your tears once more
> against this heart
> that always cries for you
> ah yes, if tears would bring
> you near to me again.
> I wish that I could almost wish you pain.

From the beginning, it was a rocky relationship. Not a good fit as some might say in today's vernacular. But at the time, he was different enough to be "cool" and had that rebel appeal that was dangerous and quirky. He wasn't "establishment" but he wasn't so far off the mainstream that I'd be breaking all of the norms of the world in which I lived. Yes, he wanted the house, the cars, and the kids but he was an artist or at least an aspiring one. And that counted for something in my inner world where conformity was something to be avoided.

For the respective families there was a problem, though. He was Jewish and I am Italian-Catholic. Neither side felt good about this arrangement. Hardly anyone had married outside their ethnic group, let alone the religion. And to make matters worse, I agreed to be married in a synagogue. I would raise our children Jewish and would practice the rituals of being a good Jewish housewife and mother. This did not go over very well with the Italian half of the family. On our wedding day, I stood with my father in the back of the synagogue preparing to walk down the aisle. The Italians were on one side and the Jews on the other. Without turning his head, my father said to me, "If you want to get out of this (marriage) I have my car parked right outside and we can leave right now. What do you think?" And I said, "Its ok Dad, I have to do this." So my father gave my hand in marriage to a man who I divorced eleven months later. A few months into the marriage, I wrote an unsent letter to my husband. It was sometime in the winter of 1970.

Dear "What's His Name":

As I am right now in a sound state of mind, I hope that these thoughts and feelings are more meaningful to me exactly one week from now at which time I must have definitely made up my mind. To go—to stay, perhaps never to return.

During this week, I must look at the overall picture in the most objective and unemotional way that I can.

Firstly, is there anything at all, the minutest thing which I like in my husband? I must think and become aware of these things because they might be the same things that attracted me to him in the first place and which might continue to hold me to him. Secondly, how many things are there that I dislike about him? Are there habits, which many people have and which may go virtually unnoticed except to my critical eye? Are his vices things which can easily be corrected, or are they habits which acquired over a given amount of years will take the same amount to correct? Am I being too critical in my evaluation of his personality and character? Do I realize that these things were there in him before we came together in marriage? Am I trying to redo him for my own personal satisfaction without realizing that he is an individual with the right to do what gives him satisfaction without always having to please someone else? If then, I truly believe in my own personal philosophy that a man must first please himself before he can attempt to please someone else—is there anything at all that can be salvaged? Is there any hope? Is my saying that I don't love you a barrier against anymore hurt, which I might incur from leaving myself open or vulnerable to your attacks? Isn't it easier to leave someone when you can say—I don't love you anymore—than to say, "I still love you but we are not compatible any more?" Our ideas were too different to start out with that it just ate away at the indefinable something, which lets people be content and happy with each other no matter what hardships might threaten to tear them apart.

What I think has happened is that you were brought up in a household where your mother was not functioning well in her role. She failed—and your father tried to pick up the pieces. You said that your father failed to straighten out your mother a long time ago and subsequently she had already done so much damage that it was too late to make any rectification. To do so, would only upset that delicate balance which threatened to ultimately destroy any semblance of a family. You said that your mother went out quite a lot and that your father had to act out the role of mother to both you and your sister. As years went by, your view of women was changed to something quite different by normal standards but frequently found in a lot of men. (These men usually find a woman who they can successfully dominate, though).

You always said that your point of view regarding women was quite old-fashioned. A woman should stay home, cook, and clean—except of course, she should work in order to help her husband—sitting home may only lead to trouble. In this way, there is no trouble because she won't get into the bit of going out—because every time she goes out and leaves you alone—it gives you the same feeling you had when your mother went out with her friends. Your neurotic habits in the house—as far as cleanliness and leaving the littlest thing out of order bring you back to your childhood—the way your mother left things on the sofa, floor, and furniture—everywhere you looked—there was dirt. You never brought your friends to your house because you were so ashamed and that's why you don't have very many friends now because you never got past the initial stages in making a friend. All these things you sub-consciously blame on your parents and you hate them for it and along with this hate you feel guilt, and this guilt drives you to overdo things—in what you do for them and what you see in them. Two years ago, you almost said that you hated them but you only got as far as saying that you felt guilty that you didn't do enough for them and in almost the same breath you said what a terrible childhood you had and that you wanted to make it up to them because of what a bad marriage they had. It sounds like you have a love-hate relationship with your partners and this somehow affects your attitudes toward me because your parents and your unhappy childhood are such an integral part of you that they are also a part of our relationship.

But even though these things are so evident to me, for instance, you want me to look perfect every time we go somewhere—not just the normal, masculine pride that a man takes in his woman—but an obsessive thing which makes me feel as though you are looking right through me. Right through the present and into the past. By now you are probably thinking—well isn't she smug—"little miss perfect" (I'll quote you) She never has anything wrong with her—it's always me". All right now, I am also thinking that this started out as a resolution to me and it turns into a letter to you. I guess it's probably because I want to discuss these things with you but as it stands that is almost virtually impossible since we would probably end up arguing.

So, I'll write about me. But more than likely it is a prejudiced opinion. No one is a very good judge of himself. Right at this time you stormed out of the apartment to tell me that I am a lousy wife because I read and write all the time—in other words, I just left you alone for 1 and ½ hours. You just told me to leave and get a divorce.

What do I always do that is wrong to you? I was trying to be rational—to write because it always helped me—and you tear it down and tell me, if you want to write—leave and become a writer—You're always writing. That's odd. Because there is nothing to show these past 11 months to say that I'm always writing—besides these few pages. There are only very short letters, which I have written to you. You always said that you admired me because I could write my thoughts out so that you could get some insight into what was troubling me and therefore come to a better understanding of our problems. But what happened, did this also get in your way, just like my music, and reacting, is this also taking me away from you?

Jo

I obtained a divorce a little over a year into the marriage. My parents had not encouraged me to leave my husband. At the time, divorce was taboo for Italian Catholics. My mother said to me, "You made your bed now go lie in it". It was a harsh reality, but there was little sympathy for young separated or divorced women.

My mother was trying to teach me with her tough love approach. Nevertheless, I left the marriage with less than a quarter of the money, clothes or other objects that I had entered with, and after a couple of months of living with my parents, my mother let it be known that I was no longer welcome to live in her house. I was on my own and it was winter. I didn't have a warm coat to wear or enough money, while legally separated, to purchase a wardrobe of clothes, or take a bus to work. My husband allowed me to leave our apartment under two conditions. I had to live at my parent's house and I could take with me only a few of my belongings. The rest had to remain behind—most of my clothes, books, records and household items. Immediately after leaving, he had the locks changed and the bank accounts frozen.

Fortunately, I worked with a woman who had a small, unused room in her apartment where I could stay until I got settled. It was an all around uncomfortable situation but as I've always found, "when one door closes, another opens" and affirms our decisions. Apparently it was time to move on, cut my losses and get on with life. For the first time I was almost completely alone.

My childhood friends had gotten on with their lives and I didn't have any close friends at that time. It was a frightening and completely uncomfortable place to be in, but in retrospect, it was the best thing that could have happened to me. I came to appreciate that I wasn't helpless, that I could take care of myself and wouldn't die from loneliness or hunger. I'd figure it out.

Some time after, I met a man where I worked who befriended me and helped me in some very significant ways. He bought me a winter coat, something I will never forget. Later on in our relationship and as we got to know one another better, he provided me with a point of view with which to envision a life that I had only dreamed was possible. He loved New York and moved there from Philadelphia shortly after I met him. Soon after I followed in his foot steps and we embarked on a life that I could never have imagined.

A few years later we married. Living in New York, I met those "big people" my father always talked about. I was on my way to building a new life in a new place meeting interesting, exciting people—where attending a Broadway show was like going to the neighborhood cinema. Dining in fine restaurants and having drinks in glamorous bars was a weekly occurrence. I met, spoke and attended parties with CEO's, Producers, Directors, and creative types—people involved with dance, arts, theatre—top attorneys, political figures and others. I attended galas, benefits and danced along side the rich and famous. The memories are strong and to this day, when I think about those times, they bring a smile to my face. I had experiences that I would never have had if I had decided to accept my circumstances and adhere to traditions that would have bound me to a very limited existence.

Almost fifteen years after divorcing my first husband, I was asked to speak at the Silent Witness Coalition, held in Trenton, New Jersey in October 1995. Victims of domestic violence were being memorialized in a public ceremony by family members. Previously I had shared the story of my first marriage with one of the professional women in the community where I lived.

I was a victim of domestic violence, having had my life threatened on more than one occasion. I was also physically and emotionally abused. The women who were planning the event were looking for a speaker who was not the perceived stereotypical victim of domestic violence—the poor white woman on welfare or a woman of color.

At the time and in that particular suburban community, there weren't many middle or upper class women who would stand in front of politicians and others to talk about their experiences with domestic violence. With much trepidation but with the support of these encouraging women, I wrote and delivered the speech.

This experience helped me to heal the emotional wounds that had been festering for so long. It helped me put the past behind me.

I was surprised by how afraid I was to speak the truth of my situation. I felt embarrassed and humiliated to have to admit that I was a victim. I was fearful that I might be found and hurt again. That is how deep the emotional wounds go. They last forever.

The best we can do is to find a way to forgive ourselves and others in a way that makes the most sense. Once again, the opportunity found me. The women who asked me to share my story had no idea how difficult it was for me to do this. How could they have known? What I've learned is that you can never fully appreciate the suffering of others. What you can do is have compassion and listen without judgment.

I'm reminded again of some of the women in my life who have profoundly impacted me. Through them came the healing and the will to move on and to help others do the same.

SILENT WITNESS SPEECH

"When I was asked to be a presenter today, I didn't hesitate to say yes. And then I got cold feet. I started thinking back to my previous marriage and my own first-hand experience with domestic violence.

It was a painful time—both physically and emotionally. So why drag those skeletons out of the closet? I guess it was time—time to reflect, re-examine, and bring out into the light of day a part of the past that is still with me.

We never know how long or deep those experiences run or how long it takes to heal the wounds to our spirit and our hearts. What, in those past experiences may still be raging within?

And so I felt it was time to talk with my son—and I was shocked by my own emotions as I shared with him the abuses I suffered. It left me drained and shaken. And he looked at me and said, "Why didn't you just leave?"

"Why didn't I leave?"

I told him that at that time and in my family divorce was a disgrace. You just didn't do it. You were married for better or worse—you were expected to handle your problems in private. This wasn't something you talked about with strangers. After all, "Aunt so and so" went through it. Who do you think you are? Are you any better than her?" There wasn't any sympathy there.

And eventually I did leave—with the clothes I was a wearing, no credit cards or bank account and few personal belongings. And I knew it was important to leave or I wouldn't live. Whether he did it or I did it—I wouldn't live.

And so, out of this re-examination process I wrote something for today that I'd like to share with you.

We must become our own witness.
Never closing ourselves off from the reality we see, hear or feel—expressing, not suppressing our emotions
Until we not only become numb to pain but joy as well
We must become our own witness and
Attempt to find our own answers to the questions
About ourselves and our lives
So that what we find not only helps ourselves
But others as well

The answers I found over the years are that I matter—we matter, I am enough—we are enough. That I live matters. That you live, matters.
Only we can bring meaning and purpose to our lives.

That it's important that we be the witnesses to our own greatness, struggles and beauty.

And in that way, any behaviors or actions that conspire to demean, belittle or threaten us are not tolerated or acceptable.

We need to be witness to our own healing, forgiveness of ourselves, our own shame, others betrayal, and other's kindness. That we love ourselves is what matters."

Standing behind me were life-sized wooden outlines of the daughters, girl friends, cousins, friends, grandmothers, mothers, and nieces of people who had died as victims of domestic violence. It was a moving and powerful image. The wooden outlines were painted blood red. In front of me, as I stood at the podium on the stairs of the New Jersey state capital building were women of all races and colors. As I spoke, they moved closer and closer together forming a tight and closed circle. They were rapt in attention and afterward followed me down the street talking with me, asking me questions and hugging me. I feel that I was not the only one who had an opportunity to heal on that day.

I had not chosen wisely in my first committed relationship. And yet I learned a lot about myself and others. Through my writing and journaling I probed my own psyche for answers. I never gave up the dream of a good and rewarding life. Perhaps I had learned from my father's mother about living with courage, faith and tenacity. Brave, strong and durable—my grandmother taught her children and their children through her deeds and actions—how to love, heal and treat others. She had endured much—infants lost in child-birth, poverty, and illiteracy—in raising her family in a foreign land. To her, the hardships, illnesses or sad feelings were not experienced as deterrents in life but as challenges to be handled. I never remember seeing or hearing my grandmother crying or throwing up her hands in despair. Instead, she prayed and asked for guidance from a power she knew and believed was bigger than her.

Unspoken Dreams

o o o o o o o o o o o o o o o o o o o o o o o o o o o o o o o o o

"Sometimes the past speaks to us through our dreams.

Might all of humankind's art, writings, films, plays, sports and what we call "entertainment" be giving voice to our ancestors dreams, fears and unfinished hopes and desires continuing through us, our children and their children?"

MY GRANDMOTHER

Giuseppa De Simone was a short, stout woman with bow legs who had a kindly and quiet gaze. She carried herself well, with back straight, and both arms perennially folded securely across her wide abdomen.

She wore small delicate earrings and her hair was always in a thin neat braided bun bound tightly in the back of her head. The ever present apron was securely tied around her waist. My grandmother was a wise, thoughtful, unschooled woman, who signed her name with an "x" and spoke no English. She neither read nor wrote in her native tongue and spoke a Neapolitan dialect.

As the matriarch of our family, we paid homage to her on holidays and at least one day of every weekend. We were the typically close Italian clan—eating, drinking and arguing together—all under her watchful eye.

My grandparents lived in a small row house in South Philadelphia with their son, my Uncle Jimmy. I didn't know my grandfather very well. Not because he wasn't alive at the time I was growing up, but because he intimidated me. I imagined there was a five foot wide circle around him and wherever he was sitting or standing. I knew not to breach that boundary. Any closer wouldn't be safe. To make matters worse, I didn't understand a word he spoke. Typically, he sat on one side of the living room area while my grandmother observed him from her perch across the room. She positioned herself on a sofa or chair by the window in the front of the house. In this way she could keep watch over him and be able to talk to the numerous neighbors who stopped by the open window to chat, exchange gossip or as they typically might do—ask for her advice or other counsel.

Years later my grandfather suffered a stroke. The dining room table was moved away and he was placed on a single bed in the far corner of the living space. He was never out of my grandmother's sight.

Giuseppa was born in Italy in the late 1880s. According to her passport, she lived in Le Castella but the family isn't certain that this information is correct. Little else of fact is known about this woman. There are few, if any, documents to mark the details of her life. People didn't keep accurate records. Birth dates and places, spelling of names, and other matters that provide context for a person's life were frequently missing or incorrect. Most of what we know about these people was written down in haste on an immigrant's papers as they embarked on their journey to America.

The personnel responsible for boarding these thousands of people onto ships were constrained by the sheer number of individuals, mostly poor and with just enough money and knowledge to get them to Ellis Island. Many of the Italian immigrants spoke various dialects of the language, some radically different. Oftentimes, they could not understand each other even though they lived in the same country. The language could vary dramatically from town to town.

The amount of missing detail from my grandmother's life piques my curiosity and gives me license to fill in the gaps. As I examine the bits and pieces left behind, a story emerges that I can hold onto about her life. I've pondered over the few recordings that marked her place on this earth. I studied entries on the Ellis Island records and noticed details such as her name, her children's names and who was responsible for her once she landed. What is missing for me is the story of why my grandmother left the motherland, what her life was like and what she saw and felt as she got closer to her destination.

On my grandmother's Alien Registration card, in the entry space marked "citizen", it reads "none" and "formerly of Italy". Her birth certificate, dated a few days before boarding the Colombo, states she was born in "Le Castella". In the Italian language, castella means "castle". Did my grandmother tell the authorities she was born in a castle? Did she create a fairy tale to explain the story of her early life in Italy?? Did she imagine herself a princess leaving her castle for a new world called America? As a stranger among people who had different customs and rules, was her task to teach them rituals and ways of seeing the world that were distinct from their own?

There have been many stories about my grandmother, most of which centered on her predictive and healing powers. She never told these stories herself, but they were recounted to me by family members who observed these activities in my grandmother's daily life. In her later years she told her daughter that God wanted her to "stop doing his work". Abruptly and with no further explanation, she no longer practiced her craft of healing and interpreting or reading people's futures.

I often wonder if her personality changed as a result. Later in her life, I sensed that she lost her spirit—becoming dour, cranky and filled with worry. Maybe there was unkind gossip about her powers or she may have become afraid of what couldn't be explained. I don't know. It may have been simply a matter of age taking its course in her life. Nevertheless, her strongest form of self-expression was denied her, either by social circumstances or innate fears—her language of healing.

My grandmother often said that I had the second sight, but that I needed to be careful as this particular gift was also a curse. People would be envious. When she visited our house she always brought me a very small hand-sewn cotton pouch. It was tightly closed with string. She said I should keep the bag close to me. I never asked her what was in the pouch nor did I attempt to open it. Her word was good enough for me. There was no need to question it. To me, she was that powerful and that wise.

Sometimes I wonder what stories were told to my grandmother by her mother and grandmother. I believe these stories comprise our mythology and legacy as her descendents. What stories might be trying to live through us now, during the days, hours and minutes of our lives? Our ancestors may be enacting their unfinished dreams and longings along side of us, as we work, shop, and live our daily routines. When we cry out in the night, awakening from a nightmare, are we participating in a dream fragment broken off from time and the past that is longing to play itself out in present generations? I imagine my female ancestors tending to their families, healing their sick, and nurturing their communities. I dream of my grandmother and great grandmother and generations living at the castle.

My grandmother practiced a ritual for as long as she was alive. She did a yearly psychic reading of her grandchildren on the eve of St. Anthony's feast day. The day before the feast she would crack open an egg and place an egg white in individual glass cups, one for each grandchild. She'd say a small prayer for each one and place them on a window ledge in the yard in the back of her house. All night the cups sat outside on the window ledge. The next morning she would "read" the egg formation which tended to crystallize and form interesting shapes. The future of that grandchild was spoken through the interpretation of that egg white. This was part of our childhood.

I can't write about my grandmother without thinking about my cousin Sofia. My cousin Sofia was the closest to having a sister of my own. I idolized Sofie, as we called her. I followed her around like a lost puppy dog. Being that she was four years older than me, I was a constant annoyance to her. And of course, when we were visiting my grandmother's house, Sofia had to take me along with her wherever she went. There are numerous pictures of me with Sofia, all of which show me looking up at her with pride and fondness. She was so different from me. I was serious, quiet and timid. Sofia was the life of every family party. She always made us laugh. I looked forward to seeing her and her mother, my Aunt Jean. There was nothing better than spending a holiday with them. The hospitality and the warmth were a balm to my soul.

Sofia spent many summers with my grandmother and Uncle Jim. She and my grandmother shared many conversations. It was as though they were two close friends. I never felt envious of their relationship, only respect and kinship with these two women. Gregarious, outgoing and lively, they added color and flavor to an otherwise sober childhood experience. Sofia didn't have an easy time of it growing up but I think it helped that our grandmother was such a kind, warm and generous soul. Maybe Giuseppa's healing powers went beyond the physical realm and affected all of us in ways that we can never know or understand.

What I know is that my grandmother, cousin and her mother loved and cherished their relationship with my father. When he passed away, a large gap appeared in the family and in all of the people's lives who he left behind. I was torn from my moorings as were others. He is still missed and spoken of frequently, especially at family gatherings. He took care of people, especially his mother, calling her every day when he got home from work until the last days of her life. When my father left the earth, he exited our lives. There has been nothing since to replace him. What we have are our memories of him.

Exits

○ ○

"Sometimes people exit our lives without advance warning or notice. My father died suddenly. During my father's last two weeks of living we hadn't spoken, because of a quarrel. We never had a chance to reconcile our differences. Then he was gone."

LETTERS OF GRIEF

Shortly after my father died I wrote two unsent letters. One was to a cousin of a close friend and the other was to my therapist who I was not seeing at the time. I'm not certain why I chose to address these two people in particular. Nonetheless, it was comforting to me to express my thoughts and feelings to them.

Dear Dick:

It's been nine months since the death of my father and the loss of someone who was not only tied to me by blood but represented something much deeper and probably more significant. I lost a friend, an ally, a supporter of my causes, and a kinsman. We held the same basic values and ideals not because they were conditioned but because they were a legacy that one has come to respect through self-evaluation, through life experiences, through learning. To inherit something one truly wants is rare indeed. It has been a very difficult time, because the lessons learned are coming to trial illuminated by the realities of a universal law. Nothing is so solid, so permanent that it will live forever. I find myself shaken by this hard and fast rule. No philosophical notion, of which I hold many, can impact an individual as powerfully as the experience of the cycle of birth, life and death. In his death at age sixty, I experience my own at age thirty-four. It was a turning point for me. I am no longer able to disillusion myself that any of my attachments are permanent. Nor will I ever feel "safe", snug, or protected. Maybe, you will think as you are reading this—why has it taken so long for this reality to sink in? I also ask myself that question. Maybe I believed in happy endings. It required a reconciliation that one can touch, feel, and see. In order for me to reconcile myself to the sudden death of a man who I have now only begun to fully appreciate is to reconcile myself with my own death and that of others whom I love and don't want to lose. Somewhere, I must find hope. Hope that there is a purpose to all of the pain and suffering we experience. Hope—that in the face-to-face encounter with terror—there is a reason to go on. And hope that we might experience joy.

There are times when I feel numb, there are times when I feel that there is no purpose, and there is no God. This is hell. I feel terror that I could lose all that I have in a second of time, as I lost my father. Joy, elation, peace are not in my realm of experiences. I fight to stay sane, to keep going, to stay afloat. But panic seizes me at times and there is no place to flee. I am faced with myself, my own destiny, my own purpose.

Jo

Dear Richard:

It is now one and one half years since the death of my father, and as you told me, I have finally accepted this is so. About a month ago, while my mother was visiting, we stopped into the New Age Bookstore in Morristown to buy a friend of mine a present to celebrate the birth of her new baby. The saleswoman informed me that a book I had ordered several months ago had arrived a week prior. She called me at home but couldn't reach me. I bought the book, took it home and asked my mother if she'd like to read it. She read some of it and said she liked what Levine was saying. That evening, she and I had dinner alone together and we started talking about my father's death and her feelings about all of this. I decided then to show her some pictures taken several weeks before he died. I had these pictures hidden away for over a year. She acknowledged them (he looked as though he were already dead) and we continued our conversation about death and dying. I told her I was trying to see death as a process, a journey where we might be reincarnated into another life or a journey into eternal peace. We had never had a conversation like this before although we have broken through the barriers in our relationship—we are now experiencing something entirely different about one another. Two days pass by and she returns to Philadelphia. She called me on a Saturday morning and told me she was ready to talk about what had happened to her the night of her conversation with me. She told me she dreamt my father came to visit her and he was very angry with her. (In all of her earlier dreams he was completely silent) He told her that he was not coming back; he was dead and she must understand this. She must go on with her life although he knew she hoped that this was all a bad dream. She told me it was so vivid a dream. His gestures and body language were so accurate she felt his presence. The next day as she was leaving and riding back on the train, she felt a tremendous sense of relief and finally renewal—a new lease on life. As for me, all dreams of him have stopped since he visited her. I feel his soul was not at peace and that we were holding him back as well as ourselves. I have been feeling lately as though I've come out of a very deep fog. The inertia, the despair has gone. My life seems fuller—more so than ever before. There are times when I feel ready to leave this world, not out of despondency, but out of joy. It is at those times when I truly feel the moment. It is at those times of peace, of letting go, that I feel free of fear and anxiety. They are also the times I feel progress and oddly enough through all of the work I continue to do on myself, I feel that maybe I will find completion in this lifetime. As you have said, there are peaks and valleys and also plains. We do get to rest in between the tough and grinding experience of working on ourselves. This process, which began with my meeting you, has not ended. It continues. You remain a voice within my consciousness—I think I am stuck with you forever. During the summer (and a time of repressing my feelings) I was choked with anxiety. And what I experienced out of all of this was the anxiety of sitting in the chair in your room when you pushed a hot button and I would feel something very intense and frightening. I realize now after having this sensation practically run me was that it was fear—fear of losing control and fear of seeing the side of me that is repressed and hidden from myself. I used to feel anger that you would deliberately want me to feel this pain—to lose control. I thought you were evil and sadistic. What I know now is that you knew that this was a powder keg ready to explode and that you would provide me with a safe place to do it. At that point, my heart made peace with you and I no longer saw you as a villain.

Jo

I hold onto these letters and they cause me to cry to this day. I remember the pain caused by writing them. I'm glad I did though. I now have them as "witness" to what can only be experienced once in a lifetime. Life intervenes and the gaps left by those we love get filled in with other important relationships.

With my son, the legacy of my father has continued. The "genes" are passed on and we can see glimpses in the seeds of the new, in a constant state of renewal and regeneration. Not all is good though—some seeds are unhealthy. On average what we can wish for is that most will thrive and grow in positive ways.

I've continued many of the same conversations I had with my father with my son who possesses many of his grandfather's traits of kindness, thoughtfulness and care of others. He's also deeply philosophical and wise.

Over the course of time, my son and I have corresponded with each other in letters, poems and emails. For better or worse, what you can say in a letter is more complete than when you attempt to speak it. It is lasting. You can read and reread what was shared and interpret its meaning according to the mood or time of day. It is "in the moment material" that has lifelong implications. The written word, unless lost or destroyed, lasts forever.

I think of the letters and poems that my son and I have shared with each other as a jazz riff. The melody is there, however subtle, punching out a rhythm. Back and forth, each note flows one into another.

That is much the way my son and I communicate—sensing as we go—discovering what each other needs to complete his or her piece of the story, the song of our life.

Learning to Grow Together

○ ○

"I wrote my son letters but rarely gave them to him. He, on the other had, wrote me letters and poems which he shared on occasions like Mother's Day and my birthday but sometimes he'd just write me a letter.

I learned about openness from my son, about sharing and giving and being myself. He was and continues to be hungry for knowledge, inquisitive and probing when necessary.

His desire for "getting to the heart of the matter" prompts me in my efforts to be a person of integrity and honesty, most especially with myself and in my dealings with others."

CONNECTIONS: JOURNAL ENTRIES AND POEMS-UNEDITED

Mom and Dad:

Being that it is now the end of the year, I felt we are all in need of some time for reflection, not only the past year, yet future years as well. The last few years have felt like a never ending roller coaster ride with transition after transition, each one taking plenty of time to be correctly focused. And, with all of the transitions I've faced, I feel I've always been able to turn around and see the same two faces. Those faces are of the both of you, my parents, and the two individuals, who together brought me into this incredible world of never ending journeys. Well, I feel like we've been through a lot together so far, high school probably being the largest triumph of them all. And through all of the arguments, most of the time followed by laughter, one most important aspect has yet to change from the both of your voices and eyes; you've never given up on me. At times, when I was ready to give up on myself, both of you were there, teaching me day after day how to succeed, no matter how many times I might have fallen, you have always amazingly been there to pick me back up. Not only have you taught me the fundamentals for succeeding and growing but about the most important characteristic in life…happiness. You may not realize it but not only do you teach me without lecturing or I prefer "discussing", but by just living out each day letting me watch your actions and then letting me have the time to soak it all in. I believe that all children have the same root regarding their relationship with their parents that helps keep one's motivational clock ticking. Not only do children or people like to feel pride for themselves; I feel it's one of the best feelings in the world to feel that one's parents feel proud of them, as individuals. And through all of my successes and failures, you've never let that feeling of pride fade away. In my life so far, I've been provided with more than many can even manage to dream. I've always had pretty much everything I've ever wanted regarding material objects. I've always had a roof over my head, with clothes on my back, "while looking damm good at the same time"…and options galore. But most importantly, I have the two of you in my life to provide me with love, and endless support.

So, this Christmas beside the traditional material gift, I want to take this time to say thank you, thank you for being the individuals you are. And I would also like to turn the issue of feeling proud around for this brief moment and tell the two of you how proud I am of you. I turn on the TV every day and watch and hear about success story after success story, yet in my eyes the two of you are the most influential success stories in my life. The climbing—the endless rota-

tions in your careers and ending up where you are today and still being juiced up for any mountain that might come your way—by consistently educating yourselves and just flat out living life to its fullest day by day. Today, I want to say that I am proud of the two of you for being who you are. So thank you both for once again being amazing and don't think that means you can stop being amazing.—This ride ain't close to being over! So, my main gift of the year of the "millennium" is an endless thank you. I am so proud to be able to look at the two of you and say, "Hey, those are my parents."

Love, Jonathan

Unsent Letter to Jonathan from Mom

Dear Jonathan:

Tonight I sit in our apartment, thinking about this day and evening twenty-one years ago when you were born. I didn't know then if I would survive the night. Like today, a nor'easter blew in. A Buddhist friend told me your birth day was a special day, all the weather elements converging. My parents were alive then. So was our good friend Lu Esther. We lived in Morristown. Now we are back in Manhattan. How weird is this? (I just had a diet meltdown, popcorn, scotch, chocolate, salsa and tacos. I wanted to celebrate.) I felt terrified on my way home from work tonight. It was terribly frightening with all kinds of debris flying around. Heavy wind gusts practically tossing you around as you walked down the street. People are so not friendly, not helping one another; it's a scary world we live in—with everyone keeping to themselves.

I am here now, deep in thought about 3/21/80 and all that led up to that day. We had moved to Morristown after living in Manhattan for seven years. We were there less than a year when I became pregnant with you. I kept my New York doctors and insisted that you would be born in New York Hospital. I had few friends in the suburbs and rarely saw my city friends. My life had changed and I didn't know enough then to build relationships and become involved in the community when we moved. So by the time I became pregnant with you I was isolated. I had problems during the pregnancy and was confined to my bed and the upstairs floor. Five months of bed rest with visits to my doctor in New York City kept me pretty much out of the loop as far as a social life was concerned. I was also trying to finish my degree. I was determined and so I had my books with me when I was admitted to the hospital. I had toxemia and it was getting bad. You were in fetal distress, my blood pressure was soaring and there were other indications that if you weren't delivered soon, both of us were in serious jeopardy. I remember every detail about that experience especially my mother losing her wallet and $400.00. Lu Ester called me as they were trying to find a vein in my arm to take blood. I remember sounding so calm. I could hear her concern and didn't want to frighten her. The wind and the rain were flooding the FDR Drive. There was thunder and lightening and it snowed. It was a wild day. I remember the ride on the stretcher to the operating floor. I continued trying to control the situation. My doctors looked frightened and the nurses could hardly hide their emotions. I tried joking with them. I didn't want them to make mistakes because they were so nervous. My heart was racing wildly though. I don't know if it was my blood pressure or from all of the excitement, the morphine, or being told that my child was in fetal distress. As I was being *prepared for surgery, I named you—Jonathan—just in case I didn't make it. I was sure you were a boy. And sure enough, you were delivered healthy, with no hormonal problems or jaundice. Your lungs were working perfectly. You were small, weighing less than 3 pounds. They said you were the miracle baby in New York Hospital's Neonatal Intensive Care Unit. Five weeks later you came home. Nine months later you were still suffering from colic, crying and screaming day and night. We had a rocky start but are determined people. And thank God, you and I are here today, safe and healthy and whole.*

Journal Entry—Jo Singel

"It was a painful day yesterday. I don't even know where to begin. Jonathan came in around 10 p.m. as white as a sheet. He didn't look well. He said he was ok and went up to his room to sleep. Don and I went shopping. We called JL on the phone, came back home to take him clothes shopping and in the car he said he didn't feel well. When we were in the store he got sick to his stomach. On the way home, I felt angry with him. He was probably up all night, did God knows what, had to sleep through the day, didn't have the presence of mind to tell me he was sick, looked unkempt, was unshaven, and then when I asked him if he had called Ron so he could mow his lawn (earn money!) he said he didn't have time. Then it blew for me, I had no mercy on him. I got on him about getting a job, not returning Doug's phone call. Last night Don spoke with him about Terry—we are concerned about this girl who can afford to call him long distance, send him presents; Jonathan is like a twirling top right now. He's in over his head; I suppose there is a pattern to this chaos.

How is my life paralleling Jonathan's? Am I being too hard on him or not hard enough? I was concerned about him all night. I couldn't sleep. I feel very disturbed by this; and yet what is "this"? This is not being responsible for the lifestyle he wants, car, spending money, making long distance phone calls. He doesn't hustle for it. He doesn't need to. For him, getting a job is a luxury, a nice thing to do. Not something he has to take seriously. He can see and talk with his friends, play most of the time. He reads very little. He hasn't bothered with anything in the house unless we ask him, with the exception of the dishes. He is a gadabout and constantly on the phone.

Who do I need to be in this situation?

What are the ground rules we can all live with here?

This is a very difficult thing, living with a teenager. No matter the circumstances parents usually, deep down blame themselves.

Journal Entry—Jonathan Singel

I sit in the classroom and look around. I see a darkness, this darkness is created, not set. It creates emptiness about the room. The sun is locked out, trying to fight its way in. The walls are bare with a desert blue. Nothing hangs for my personal view. I look around and see many eyes. These eyes stare, that's all they do. They don't know what to look at; they don't know what to do. A chalkboard hangs on the wall ahead where prints are made. Prints of white are written all over, the eyes watch these prints as if they were holy. They give direction, these white prints do, for a source of knowledge, they help with that too. A woman stands ahead, with a strict way about her, she watches the eyes as if they were gold, every once in awhile she mutters a word to discipline the eyes to a perfect mold. The eyes obey, that's all they can do for if they don't then there would be just a few. The lights are bright, filling the room with a sucking white. It pulls at your eyes as if they were food. The chairs and desks reflect something cold. They open up like mouths and eat your materials, the materials that you use to complete your day. Work is done and accomplishment is rewarded. These eyes act in fear, that's all they know. The door remains closed, so distraction is locked away, if it exists the loss of knowledge might persist. These eyes they watch, in a room with no view, they watch because it's all they can do.

Letter to Mom from Jonathan

Dear Mom,

This letter is being addressed to you for a certain purpose. That purpose is to explain to you why I am not doing my schoolwork in a satisfactory or above satisfactory fashion. I do know that I talk a lot of stuff about getting better grades and what I have to do. I know and you know by what I have said that I know what I need to do in order to earn better grades. I understand fully what my weaknesses are in my school habits and what I have to do in order to improve them and get better grades. In a couple of words, basically I just have to put forth the effort and do my best. But I am obviously not putting forth my best effort. The obvious reason is because I just don't want it enough. That's true in every single aspect in life. It all comes down to who wants it the most. The people who want it the most do succeed. I just don't want it enough. I do fully understand that every single day that I go to school I am shaping my future and building my own pathway. So far that pathway has been very messy. There is something in me that is just not turning on when I walk into that classroom or start my homework. That motivation just isn't there. I understand that is a very serious thing. I talk the talk but I don't walk the walk. You and dad have been extremely helpful in every twist and turn in my life. You have coached me to do better and worked with me on your free time in order to help me create that special and very important pursuit of excellence in my life. But, obviously that just isn't good enough, because you're doing your part but I'm just not doing mine.

I want it, but sadly enough I don't. It just hasn't hit me hard enough yet that my future as an adult is just around the corner, but if I don't shape up, that future isn't going to be too pretty. When I walk into the school doors, I am not mentally energized to do my best and work hard. Instead, I walk in the school doors like a bum with my eyes half closed. But, you can count on this, for the next several days I am going to do some large thinking about my future and decide who and where I want to be. I know I am too darn smart to let this pass by. I know God didn't put me on this earth to be a street bum and not succeed. Trust me; I am not planning on letting him or myself down. Tonight, the night in which I am typing up this letter for you is the most pumped up I have been about doing well on my school work for a long, long time. I will not be forced to make a rocky road for my future or quit the track team. Because, both of those things mean too much to me right now.

So, you can expect to see a big change in Jonathan Singel as a young adult and a human being on this planet earth in the next couple of weeks. I will not let you or myself down. In two weeks my grades will be improved and I will be on the track team. I do want to say think you to you and dad for putting so much of your time and energy into helping me improve my grades. I am just sorry that I didn't fill my half of the bargain. I will make it up not only for you but also for myself. I will be pressing those buttons from now on and going that extra mile to do better. I'm sure the buttons will be a little rusty, but they will be oiled and pressed. For the next couple weeks I will be looking at this saying which will be posted on my bedroom wall and I plan to live by it for the rest of my life. I will sign it as if it is a contract in which I live by its wise words…

Love, Jonathan

Poem by Jonathan Singel

So sad no matter how vile...
Reckless people I see every other mile...
A cure that we don't seem to find...
Sadness has invaded all our minds...
The world calls us as we turn our backs...
Mother earth has experienced too many setbacks...
Mother earth suffers from a disease called greed...
Because, many feel that there's no longer a need...
My gratitude to those who've tried...
To keep this world, a world of pride...
And shame on those who for this world don't mind...
This world, this place, doesn't need those kind...
Little we see in nature that is ours...
A setting, a world, a place that's seen too many fires

Diary for My Unborn Son

I wrote these diary entries while in bed, several months pregnant and growing increasingly sick with approaching toxemia. If I had not lived, they would have been my legacy. I didn't share them with anyone but kept my growing fears for my unborn child's safety to myself.

As I recorded each day's events, I sensed who he was and who he was going to be. He became more real and alive to me although he was in grave danger. I had no tests but knew he was a boy, so I named him Jonathan Lawrence after two of our closest friends whom he now considers his unofficial "uncles", John and Larry. We chose his name, one evening, while dining with our good friend, Lu Esther Mertz at the United Nations Plaza. Sitting around the beautiful table facing a dazzling New York skyline, I looked at our two handsome friends and said, "I know his name. I want him to have both of your names." And so it was.

> ### February 16, 1980
> *I believe that a part of our mind foresees the entire course of a relationship before we begin it, and we choose to enter that series of events as the gentlest possible way to learn the lessons we are now ready to learn.*
> *Everything that happens between two people is by mutual design. Although this is usually not seen at the moment, it is often recognized later.*
>
> ### February 26
> *Who, but the poets tell of the lives of people—*
> *dawdlers, visionaries that they are.*
>
> ### March 4
> *Many nights pass. I feel my aloneness. Reach out, touch, and see that you are not alone.*
>
> ### March 6
> *It's my birthday today.*
> *No celebrating for me. The diet doesn't permit anything fun to eat.*
> *Mom and Dad are here.*
> *I'm feeling a little down. Self-pity is a very depressing thing.*
>
> ### March 16
> *Are you there? Not wanting to attach myself to you. Not hoping. Maybe I should allow myself to be with you. If only for a short time. Precarious situation. I do talk to you, encouraging you, we are in this together. Maybe it's harder for you. I'd like you to survive, if only because you have been given existence in my life. No, you*

don't have a name, that's ok. You see, I don't want to hurt too much. I'm trying to communicate with you. Are you there? I love you, it's ok, you do what you must do. I'll understand. It would be nice though to find out who you are.

March 18
The doctor wants to see me in a couple of days. If things get worse, I'll be going to the hospital.
If only I can hold out a little longer so that you have a chance to grow.
I had another sonogram; you're still there, at least.

March 19
I'll be going to the doctor tomorrow.
I'm so afraid of losing you…losing me.
Trying to relax is very difficult.

March 20
I arrived at the hospital.
BP is 160/110—or thereabouts.
It doesn't look good for us.
Had a fetal stress test; you're in trouble.

March 21
You were born today.
Under rather adverse circumstances I'm afraid.
My BP arose to over 200.
An emergency cesarean was performed at 9 p.m.
The doctor said you emerged a bouncing baby.
They whisked you past your father and carried you to the intensive care unit.
All 3 lbs.
It was cold, snowy, raining hurricane weather like day. According to a Buddhist it was a day when all four seasons met. A holy day.

March 22
Well, it looks as though you've arrived 2 months early. But you're doing well.
I spent this weekend in a labor room, very sick.
Your dad was with me the whole time.

March 23
Left intensive care. You're doing well.
Your dad loves visiting you.
As soon as he enters the hospital he's running to see you.
I'm unable to leave my bed.
So our meeting will have to wait.

March 30
You're doing fine; I'm getting anxious to leave here.

April 1
Homecoming day for me.
First day of the transit strike.
I'm leaving you in the hospital today. I didn't say goodbye.
It snowed in Morristown. I wasn't in a very good mood.
Mom and Dad came to take care of me.
Adjusting to a new life is very difficult.

May 12
People pick their own time to be born.
What does the future hold for someone with so tempestuous a beginning?

May 13
Your grandparent's town was hit by a tornado. Their arrival has been delayed. It's a terribly ugly day.
I spoke with my mother and father today.
He told me that my son would protect me when he grows up…from the things I'm afraid of.
Do I need you to protect me?
Is there truth in the oedipal complex?

I also spoke to my best friend about you; we think you're someone special.
She thinks you can't help but be special—I am special and so are you.

May 14
Grandparents Singel and great grandmother Singel arrived today. You absolutely fascinate them. I never thought your grandfather would show as much affection for you as he does. He talks to you and you seem to listen to him. Your grandfather wants to be listened to. They are tending to your needs. You and I are having a vacation from each other.

May 15
You were to be born today. Instead you had a head start. What effect has that had on you? You seem very afraid as though the world and its people will not to be trusted. Is this inherited or just a natural occurrence. There were visitors today.

May 16
A good friend came out for the weekend. My family is still here. We made wonderful fettuccine Alfredo tonight.
Your grandparents are not so accustomed to our ways. Will we be to yours? It's the whole question of flexibility, Jonathan. I'm seeing the importance of it. Everyone remarks how good you are. We've already had our moments, you and I.

May 17
It was a good day today.
The experience of having you has helped me see the world in a different way.

May 24
How are you going to feel about the city?
Will you enjoy it as much as we do?
You seem to be very strong willed and assertive.

May 26
You seem to be more attentive to me.
Memorizing my face—staring at me as I feed you.

To Mom from Jonathan on her 50ᵗʰ Birthday

Who is that woman?
Who is that woman who works?
Who is that woman who cares?
Who is that woman who forgives?
Who is that woman who understands?
Who is that woman that educates?
Who is that woman that learns?
Who is that woman that loves?
A strong woman she is
For that woman goes all day long
Not long that she waits
To laugh and to cry
A laugh of many years
A tear of many moons
Who is that woman?
That woman is strong
That woman is stable
That woman is a mother
A mother then
A mother there
A mother now
Who is that woman?
That woman is my mother

Turning "50"

○ ○

"When I turned fifty years old, the song changed and a new one began to hum itself into existence."

LETTERS TO MYSELF

Turning fifty didn't suddenly bring relief or resolution to the open questions I had been living with—mostly revolving around "what will make me happy" and "what will bring me peace of mind". Maybe the way in which I depicted my struggles during the first fifty years changed, but for the most part, if I'm honest, what was really different? Only as I get close to "60" do I see progress toward being someone who doubts less, loves more, and takes life on its own terms with less need for control and more give and take.

Journal Entry—March 1999

"I'm learning a lot in these last few days before I am fifty years old. And learning doesn't always come without pain. It involves holding onto an experience long enough so that you can breakthrough to the other side of it. Sustaining the tension is hard. There's a tendency to make the discomfort go away.

In the area of relationships, well, once in awhile there comes along someone who you feel so at home with, it's like your soul has found a resting place, time seems to stand still for while. When I find someone who I feel this connection with, I don't want to leave. I cling, instead of continuing the flow. I try to set it into stone.

I think I get confused in those moments. The "person" becomes the means to having more of these moments—just as a trainer might wish a seminar or work-shop to never end—or a participant wants that experience to continue versus hold-ing it in their heart and moving on.

I've tried to capture those moments—always in vain—just as we try to capture images in pictures—on film—so we can evoke the memories—we dislike letting go—having the experience—allowing what's next to unfold.

Permanent friends—people who come with you throughout life—we try to cre-ate tribes—for safety—fearing to travel alone—and yet we are alone—no one can get inside me—here in my skin—I want to let go of the tribe and yet I can't quite get there. I leave—return—leave—return—I don't hold the tension long enough—when I return, I come back because I've lost my way, feel lost, lonely, needy, wanting something I can't ever name—not getting it—feeling angry, more lost. I leave—seek again—don't find what I'm searching for—come back.

I never really left home.

I clung—I cling.

I don't go back feeling whole—but wanting something. At home, they are baf-fled by my behavior.

I need to leave home, symbolically, and return whole, giving.

Who do I genuinely want to talk with, be with? Probably, the people I know and like at work.

I have the feeling that when I let go—I will let in some interesting people. Will I be lonely when or if I ever get old? If I continue to feel lonely now—I will—or if I continue to cling and not let go of the past—or if I continue to project out into the future—there will be more of the same, no doubt.

I keep trying to organize my life—as if it will somehow help me tie up all the loose ends. Getting everything lined up won't work. I think sometimes I don't realize that I've changed and then get angry because others haven't. Then I feel shut out. I need to recognize my own change. When others close to me don't change with me, I feel alone.

Like at home growing up—I kept growing.

Most of the people around me stayed the same for a long time.

I felt shut out—they felt I was aloof, condescending.

Most people aren't motivated to change, grow, and learn at the rate at which I want. It's scary on both sides. Sometimes, I can't keep up with myself.

I'm too caught up in needing to be validated, looking to others for answers.

I need to live in my own questions, learning, learning, all the time.

Staying awake—it ain't easy.

But who said it would be?

Journal Entry—February 1999

"There probably has never been a time when I haven't mentally or physically struggled with something. I've been immature my whole life. I've had a difficult time with self-control, focus, commitment, and intimacy. This life has been a long, hard struggle, wrestling with so many demons. There have been few times of feeling a sense of inner peace. That I can remember them shows how infrequent they were.

At this point, less than a month into turning 50, I've had glimmers of what this inner peace can feel like. For me, it's just being in the moment, accepting what is there, as is, and not trying to change it. I know I need to have acceptance of myself, in order to arrive at acceptance of others.

My discontent has caused pain to others. If I can forgive myself for causing others pain, maybe I can arrive at forgiving others for the pain they have caused me.

I read the other day that what we try to do is have a life of happiness, we are happy when there is no strife or conflict or pain. If that's what we're waiting for, well, then there's no chance of being happy. I think of the movie, "Life is Beautiful". It's about savoring the moments, wherever you are, no matter what the conditions of your life.

I think I've been trying to paint that perfect picture of what a good life should be about. Living in the conversation of, "if only there were...if only there were...more time, more money, more friends, more clothes..." But "if only" never arrives. On the sunniest of days a sudden thundershower can occur and you're caught without an umbrella or raincoat. A swarm of bees can descend on your picnic. An ant hill, quietly slumbering, awakens and invades your food. The wine can spill, a bee can sting, what will you do? Will it ruin your whole day? Will it run your life? Were you hoping that it would be a perfect day? Are you hoping for a perfect life? Are you willing to accept the mishaps, the surprises and not be upset by them? But to turn whatever happens into opportunities? Will a beautiful butterfly appear out of nowhere? Will a bird you've never seen or heard before make its presence known? Will someone tell a funny joke or a story of an adventure that makes you laugh out loud? Will you be present enough or distracted by the unexpected? How do you want to live your life? Is the glass half-empty? Or is it half full?

Nineteen years ago to this day, I was lying in an intensive care unit, in great pain and discomfort, having given birth to my son. Returning to my hospital room with very high blood pressure, I was a complete mess. Blood covered my teeth. I felt completely in shambles. The day I finally got out of bed was a hard, hard day. And here I am today, my son at college, my husband at work, my parents' deceased, comfy and snug sitting in my living room, enjoying my hot cup of coffee. How little we know what life will bring us. What I know now is that our attitude means a lot, how we handle what shows up, more than the event, stays with us forever, shapes and molds us.

Our life experiences, not the events, but our interpretation of those events, is what is important. How we experience life, how we respond to the stuff that happens determines the quality and maybe even the quantity of our lives. The fullness *of our experience, how much of life we are willing to let in is up to each one of us. Fear will block out much of the richness of our life experience.*

Looking at life through fearful eyes will make us timid and limit our resourcefulness and opportunities. How does your fear of things limit you? Who do you fear? What do you fear? What do you need to do to confront those fears? Will you leave the picnic site and explore other areas? Or, are you too tired, comfortable, and afraid?

To The Future

○ ○

"A few years ago my son asked me to write a letter to my future grandchildren.

I complied and as I did it sent me down a path of reflection, of looking back from the future, talking to my grandchildren from the past, hoping to hand down the seeds, the thoughts, the ideas for the dream to continue."

TO MY GRANDCHILDREN, AS YET UNBORN

Children, the best you can do is to do your best—to approach life from the perspective that you have within you the resources, the power, the knowledge, the skills to look around you, to critically and honestly assess your situation, to choose, and to decide what it is that you can do to contribute to what you believe in, what you cherish and hold true. Most importantly, decide what is the "righteous" path for you to walk—that would do no harm to you or others—that would respect life, this life—not an after-life—but this life we know and that we are living now.

Look within yourself first—what does your heart say? Does it say "take from others so that you can have more than they do?" If so, I'd ask you to consider what will result from that way of thinking and acting? Will you be happier having more than others? Will that make you feel satisfied with your life?

Will your life have more value as a result? Will your children respect and honor you? What will your children learn from you?

When you look deeper into your heart, what else does it say? Does it say, "Lock your doors, lock your heart and don't listen to the cries of another?" Does it say, turn-off, tune out, shut up, be quiet, don't say anything, and be afraid? What does it say? Does it say don't stand out, look like everyone else, don't rock the boat or people will think you are crazy, mad, and full of nonsense?

Children—what will you hear when you listen to what your heart wants to say? Do it now before it is too late. Do it before you are too old or unaware that your heart speaks to you everyday. Don't believe the adults around you when they tell you that you are too young to know what you know. Hold onto your innocence, your curiosity. Listen to me, your grandmother. Your heart is bigger and more powerful than your mind. Your heart knows the song that you were born to sing. Your heart knows all that you will ever need to know and that it will break if you don't listen to its song.

You know more than I will ever know—now in this time of your life when you have not yet been taught to be afraid to listen to your heart. Children, put your right hand over your heart and tell me what it is saying to you. And I say, children, follow what your heart says. It is the one true thing you can count on. Use this gift that every person born into the world has—no matter how rich or poor, or what country they are born into, or what language they speak or what religion they follow. Everyone has a heart. Follow it with confidence.

Epilogue

As I close this story I think about my Uncle Jimmy, who, not too long before he died, said to a gathering of his nieces and nephews, "I want you to all love one another. You hear?" Simple, straight-forward and direct, Uncle Jimmy wasted little time in getting to his point.

Uncle Jimmy had called his nieces and nephews together at a family reunion at my Cousin Sofia's house. He had just given each of us a small monetary gift. He wanted us to have something to remember him by while he was still alive. Perhaps he knew at the time that he was very ill. He also knew that each of us, in our once close knit Italian family, was having issues with one another. The rest of his inheritance to us would be distributed after his death.

Uncle Jimmy was a short, small man. He always gave his nieces and nephews a few dollars every time he visited their homes. He was a quiet man with one pleasure—Camel's, un-filtered cigarettes, which were considered a permanent part of him. Wherever he was, you could count on there being a steady stream of smoke.

Another love of his was his car, a four-door, massive hunk of steel with a V-8 engine, which he drove like a cowboy riding a bull. His head would barely reach above the back of the seat while his small arms wrapped themselves tightly around the large steering wheel. After family get-togethers at our house on Woodlawn Avenue, we'd stand back far away from the curb and watch in amazement as he floored the gas pedal and drove off in a blaze of smoke; an impressive exit for such a little man!

That was our Uncle Jimmy. God bless his soul. His generosity wasn't in his monetary gifts but in his good-natured and heart-felt attempt to share with us what he had to offer.

After all of these passing years, it is the words of this uneducated, yet wise, man that have lasted, "You all love one another. You hear?"

Afterword

For the dreamer in all of us...

If you've ever made a wish on a dandelion and trusted the wind to carry your dreams to distant places, know you are not alone but need to shout out those wishes so that others can hear you.

Don't keep those dreams to yourself. Be joyful and passionate as you express your deepest desires.

Call attention to yourself in a respectful way. No one will know you exist until you tell them and show them who you are.

Find your voice and true self but do it soon because there is no time to waste. Don't ever give up or give in to who the world wants you to be. Fully express yourself in ways that are unique to your own talents and personality. Bring those special qualities to everything that you do. You don't have to imitate, copy, or envy others.

You have enough natural talents that would fill a lifetime and beyond. So begin now.

Don't be stingy with yourself. Whatever you share do it freely and without thought of return. Whatever you give will come back to you fourfold. Maybe you will not receive from the same source but in unexpected and surprising ways.

Above all else, stand for something big and bold and give it everything you've got. There will be many times when you will not feel embraced in the dream you have for yourself or your world. People around you may be afraid of how you might want them to change. They're not the one who needs to change, it's you. Focus on yourself. It's ok to be selfish and self-centered about this.

For too long and too often the quiet and the unassuming people have acted afraid and in meek and humble ways. The world needs every one of us and all of the dreams we have for it.

Don't settle for anything less than who you are and what you want. Each of us is connected to and impacts one another. Whatever you do or say has an effect on someone else. Many times, you will never know how you have influenced someone else or inspired or been an example.

Your courage, tenacity, and perseverance add one more ounce of goodness to the world and to humanity. Trust that everything else will follow. You will stand as a role model for someone who is struggling to be true to themselves. In turn, you will find immense pleasure and satisfaction in knowing that you have made a difference in another person's life.

It's alright to admit you don't know something or need to learn. It's not a sign of weakness but just the opposite. Too often we think we need to do it alone, afraid to admit our ignorance or lack of knowledge and wisdom.

Discover who supports you in your greatness. Accept nothing less and let go of the rest.

Honor the warrior, the saint, the sinner, and the hero or heroine in yourself. It's all there waiting to be used. Use it all up—your talents, skills, and experiences in service of something bigger. Tell your stories. Be open to all that life has to offer. Treasure it all.

Be afraid and do whatever it is that may be keeping you that one centimeter away from your greatness. I support you in your greatness as I would like you to support me in mine.

978-0-595-36092-5
0-595-36092-0

9 780595 360925